Sweet Vegan

Nicole Maree

Sweet Vegan

Nicole Maree

Hardie Grant

BOOKS

Published in 2020 by Hardie Grant Books, an imprint of Hardie Grant Publishing

Hardie Grant Books (Melbourne)
Building 1, 658 Church Street
Richmond, Victoria 3121

Hardie Grant Books (London)
5th & 6th Floors
52–54 Southwark Street
London SE1 1UN

hardiegrantbooks.com

 A catalogue record for this
book is available from the
National Library of Australia

Sweet Vegan
ISBN 978 1 74379 646 7

Publisher: Pam Brewster
Project Editor: Margaret Bowman/Loran McDougall
Editor: Allison Hiew
Design Manager: Mark Campbell/Jessica Lowe
Cover designer: Mietta Yans
Text designer: Michelle Mackintosh
Photographers: Elisa Watson, Jeremy Butler
Stylist: Georgia Young
Production Manager: Todd Rechner
Colour reproduction by Splitting Image Colour Studio
Printed in China by Leo Paper Products LTD.

Lovingly dedicated to Jeremy.
I thank you
for all the sacrifices you have made
for your support and guidance
for your love and laughter
for your encouragement and motivation
for being there for me always
but most of all, thank you for making me ridiculously happy.
I love you, always and forever. x

Contents.

Introduction.

My most treasured memories start in the kitchen: Grandma's cookies, Mum's 'special occasion' caramel tart and Dad's spicy fruitcake. Each warm aroma, texture and flavour hints at the love, time and family history poured into each dish.

Family time for me has always involved baking. The moments when we gather in one place and bring something special to the table. It's about breaking bread and sharing all our highs and lows. It's how I connect with the people I love and treasure the most.

So after years of battling food intolerances and having a strong love for desserts, I was forced to perfect the art of converting sweet recipes into indulgent creations that are vegan and free from dairy, gluten and nuts. These were old recipes, made new, that I could enjoy alongside my friends and family.

Sweet Vegan will transform your kitchen from the inside out, showcasing recipes that ooze, crunch, crumble and melt just like their originals. You'll learn to sneak vegetables into cheesecakes, fruit into delightful desserts, and how to make your own chocolatey goodness.

As well as sharing my own creations, I'll guide you in substituting dairy, eggs, sugar, flour, oil and nuts, so you can easily adapt your favourite sweets. Whether you're vegan, have a food allergy or intolerance, or simply want to learn how to transform indulgent recipes for friends with different dietary requirements, this book is for you. I hope you'll be inspired to use the lessons here to create your own path and author your own recipes.

Love what you bake. Turn up the tunes and dance in the kitchen. Laugh and share your bench with friends and family. Create a terrible mess of batter and don't take it too seriously. Food is a precious gift. It's life on a plate, and it's far too delicious not to share.

Lots of love from the kitchen,
Nicole Maree

MINI
TREATS

RUMMY RAISIN TREATS

DAIRY FREE, GLUTEN FREE, VEGAN

Blend 100 g (3½ oz) of the desiccated coconut with all the remaining ingredients except the raisins in a food processor until the mixture is combined and starts to stick together. Transfer to a large bowl and fold in the raisins.

Take a tablespoon of the mixture, form it into a ball and roll it in the remaining coconut. Repeat with the remaining mixture.

Transfer the treats to an airtight container and refrigerate for 1 hour to set.

Store in an airtight container in the fridge for up to 1 week or in the freezer for up to 2 months.

Makes 22 treats

140 g (5 oz) unsweetened desiccated coconut
140 g (5 oz) medjool dates, pitted
200 g (7 oz) dry-roasted unsalted cashew nuts (see note)
20 g (¾ oz) coconut oil, softened
30 g (1 oz/¼ cup) cacao powder
25 ml (¾ fl oz) sweet rum
50 g (1¾ oz) raisins

NOTE
For a nut-free variation, you can replace the cashew nuts with gluten-free arrowroot biscuits.

TAHINI TREATS

DAIRY FREE, GLUTEN FREE, NUT FREE, VEGAN

I adore these snacks and keep them on standby in the freezer. They're perfect for those late-night sweet cravings or a mid-morning energy boost.

Blend 80 g (2¾ oz) of the desiccated coconut with all the remaining ingredients in a food processor until the mixture is combined and starts to stick together.

Transfer to a large bowl and freeze for 30 minutes to firm up.

Take a heaped tablespoon of the mixture, form it into a ball and roll it in the remaining coconut. Repeat with the remaining mixture.

Transfer the treats to an airtight container and freeze for 15 minutes to set.

Store in an airtight container in the fridge for up to 1 week or in the freezer for 2 months.

Makes 20 treats

110 g (4 oz) unsweetened desiccated coconut
220 g (8 oz) hulled tahini
80 ml (2½ fl oz/⅓ cup) maple syrup
80 g (2¾ oz) currants
50 g (1¾ oz/⅓ cup) sesame seeds
80 g (2¾ oz) dried dates, finely chopped
80 g (2¾ oz) dried apricots, diced

HUNNYCOMB

DAIRY FREE, GLUTEN FREE, NUT FREE, VEGAN

Line the base and sides of a 30 cm × 20 cm × 3.5 cm deep (12 in × 8 in × 1½ in) slice tin with baking paper.

For the hunnycomb, melt the coconut sugar, butter and brown rice syrup in a deep saucepan over a low heat. Once melted, increase the heat to medium and bring to the boil. Boil, without stirring, for 5 minutes.

Remove from the heat and add the bicarbonate of soda, stirring quickly for a few seconds until the mixture is combined and foaming.

Pour the mixture carefully onto the prepared slice tin and leave to set and cool for 15 minutes. Freeze for another 15 minutes, then remove the hunnycomb from the tin and break it into pieces using a sharp knife.

For the chocolate, add 5 cm (2 in) water to a large saucepan and bring to the boil over a medium–high heat. Set a medium glass or ceramic mixing bowl on top, making sure the mixing bowl isn't touching the water. Add the cacao buttons to the mixing bowl and melt for about 3 minutes. Once melted, whisk in the maple syrup until combined.

Turn off the heat and set the bowl on a flat surface. Add the cacao powder and vanilla extract and whisk until smooth.

Drizzle the chocolate over the hunnycomb and refrigerate until the chocolate has set.

Store in an airtight container in the fridge for 1 week or in the freezer for up to 1 month.

Serves 12

HUNNYCOMB
180 g (6½ oz) coconut sugar
20 g (¾ oz) vegan butter
50 g (1¾ oz) brown rice syrup
2 teaspoon bicarbonate of soda

CHOCOLATE
50 g (1¾ oz) cacao butter buttons
20 ml (¾ fl oz) pure maple syrup
10 g (¼ oz) cacao powder
¼ teaspoon vanilla extract

CREAMY EGGS

DAIRY FREE, GLUTEN FREE, VEGAN

Line two 38 cm × 25 cm (15 in × 10 in) baking trays (cookie sheets) with baking paper.

For the cream, soak the cashew nuts in boiling water for 1 hour.

Drain the cashew nuts, rinse well and add to a high-speed blender or food processor along with the vanilla extract, maple syrup, coconut butter and sea salt. Blend until very smooth.

Place about two-thirds of the cashew nut mixture in a separate bowl. To the remaining third of the mixture, add the tahini, turmeric and dates and blend well. Transfer to a separate bowl. Cover both mixtures and freeze for 1 hour or until firm.

Once firm, wet your hands – this will make the processes so much easier! Roll a teaspoon of the turmeric filling into a ball. Press a small amount of the cream filling around the turmeric filling to form an egg shape. Place on the prepared baking tray. Repeat with the remaining mixture. Freeze the eggs for 2 hours.

When the eggs are nearly ready, make the chocolate. Add 5 cm (2 in) water to a large saucepan and bring to the boil over a medium–high heat. Set a medium glass or ceramic mixing bowl on top, making sure the mixing bowl isn't touching the water. Add the cacao buttons to the mixing bowl and melt for about 3 minutes. Once melted, whisk in the maple syrup until combined. Turn off the heat, remove the bowl and set on a flat surface.

Whisk in the cacao powder and vanilla extract until smooth.

Dip an egg into the chocolate to coat, then remove with two forks. Repeat with the remaining eggs, placing each coated egg on the prepared baking tray. Refrigerate for 30 minutes, until the chocolate has set.

Store in an airtight container in the fridge for 1 week or in the freezer for up to 1 month.

Makes 10 eggs

CREAM

150 g (5½ oz/1 cup) raw
  cashew nuts
½ teaspoon vanilla extract
65 ml (2¼ fl oz) maple syrup
30 g (1 oz) coconut butter, melted
⅛ teaspoon sea salt
1 teaspoon hulled tahini
⅛ teaspoon ground turmeric
2 soft medjool dates, pitted

CHOCOLATE

200 g (7 oz) cacao butter buttons
85 ml (2¾ fl oz) pure maple syrup
50 g (1¾ oz) cacao powder
1 teaspoon vanilla extract

LEMON & TURMERIC BALLS

DAIRY FREE, GLUTEN FREE, NUT FREE, VEGAN

Blend 140 g (5 oz) of the sunflower kernels with all the remaining ingredients in a food processor until the mixture is combined and starts to stick together.

Freeze the mixture for 15 minutes or until firm. Finely chop the remaining sunflower kernels.

Once the mixture is firm, take a tablespoon of the mixture, form it into a ball and roll it in the chopped sunflower kernels. Repeat with the remaining mixture.

Transfer the treats to an airtight container and freeze for 1 hour to set.

Store in the freezer in an airtight container for up to 2 months.

Makes 22 balls

220 g (8 oz) raw sunflower kernels

60 ml (2 fl oz/¼ cup) rice malt syrup

150 g (5½ oz) medjool dates, pitted

55 g (2 oz) unsweetened desiccated coconut

80 g (2¾ oz) dried apricots, roughly chopped

2 teaspoons chia seeds

1 teaspoon finely grated lemon zest

30 ml (1 fl oz) freshly squeezed lemon juice

1 teaspoon vanilla extract

½ teaspoon ground ginger

½ teaspoon ground turmeric

20 g (¾ oz) coconut oil, softened

CHOCOLATE CRACKLES

DAIRY FREE, GLUTEN FREE, NUT FREE, VEGAN

Line a standard twelve-cup muffin tin with silicone muffin cases.

In a high-speed blender or food processor, blend the coconut sugar and arrowroot starch on a low speed and gradually increase to high speed over 1 minute or until the mixture has a powdered-sugar texture. Let the mixture settle for 1 minute before removing the lid. Set aside.

Add 5 cm (2 in) water to a large saucepan and bring to the boil over a medium–high heat. Set a medium glass or ceramic mixing bowl on top, making sure the mixing bowl isn't touching the water. Add the cacao buttons to the mixing bowl and melt for about 3 minutes.

In a large bowl, combine the coconut sugar mixture, cacao powder, rice cereal and desiccated coconut well. Pour over the melted cacao mixture and stir to combine.

Spoon the crackle mix evenly into the prepared muffin tin. Set in the fridge for 1 hour.

Store in an airtight container in the fridge for 1 week or in the freezer for up to 1 month.

Makes 16 large crackles

125 g (4½ oz) coconut sugar
½ tablespoon arrowroot starch
250 g (9 oz) cacao butter buttons
60 g (2 oz) cacao powder
200 g (7 oz) puffed rice cereal
100 g (3½ oz) desiccated coconut

MINT-AS FUDGE

DAIRY FREE, GLUTEN FREE, NUT FREE, VEGAN

Line the base and sides of a 17 cm × 17 cm (6¾ in × 6¾ in) cake tin with baking paper, ensuring the paper hangs over the sides of the tin for easy removal.

For the chocolate swirl, heat the condensed milk, sugar, maple syrup and coconut butter in a saucepan over a medium–low heat. Cook, stirring, without boiling for 5 minutes or until the sugar has dissolved.

For the mint swirl, heat the condensed milk, maple syrup and coconut butter in a saucepan over a medium–low heat. Cook, stirring, without boiling until all the ingredients are melted.

Remove each saucepan from the heat. To the chocolate swirl saucepan add the chocolate and mix well, until the chocolate is melted. To the mint swirl saucepan add the cacao butter, peppermint extract and spirulina (for colour) and mix well until combined.

Working quickly, spoon dollops of both mixtures into the prepared tin, alternating between the two colours. Using a skewer, swirl the two together to create a marble effect. Freeze for 2 hours to set.

Remove from the tin, discard the baking paper and slice into pieces.

Store the fudge in an airtight container in the freezer for up to 1 month.

Makes 30 pieces

CHOCOLATE SWIRL
80 g (2¾ oz/¼ cup) coconut
   condensed milk
35 g (1¼ oz) coconut sugar
35 ml (1¼ fl oz) maple syrup
75 g (2¾ oz) coconut butter
70 g (2½ oz) vegan milk chocolate,
   roughly chopped

MINT SWIRL
115 g (4 oz/½ cup) coconut
   condensed milk
35 ml (1¼ fl oz) maple syrup
75 g (2¾ oz) coconut butter
70 g (2½ oz) vegan raw
   cacao butter (see note)
1 teaspoon peppermint extract
½ teaspoon spirulina powder

NOTE
You can use vegan white chocolate in place of cacao butter.

NEAPOLITAN FUDGE

DAIRY FREE, GLUTEN FREE, NUT FREE, VEGAN

This is for my siblings, Katanya and John. In our house there were never any arguments about Neapolitan ice cream. Kat would steal the strawberry, and John would scoop from the chocolate. Me? I'd always try to take from all three!

Line the base and sides of a 10.5 cm × 20 cm (4¼ in × 8 in) loaf (bar) tin with baking paper.

For the chocolate layer, put the condensed milk, sugar, maple syrup and coconut butter in a saucepan over a medium–low heat. Cook, stirring, without boiling for 5 minutes or until the sugar has dissolved. Remove from the heat and add the chocolate. Mix well until the chocolate is melted. Working quickly, spoon into the prepared loaf tin and smooth the top. Freeze for 30 minutes.

For the strawberry layer, purée the strawberries in a blender. Strain the purée through a fine-mesh sieve, reserving the liquid. Discard the pulp and put the liquid, condensed milk, sugar, maple syrup and coconut butter in a saucepan over a medium–low heat. Cook, stirring, without boiling for 5 minutes or until the sugar has dissolved. Remove from the heat and add the white chocolate. Mix well until the chocolate is melted. Working quickly, evenly spoon the mixture on top of the chocolate layer, smoothing the top. Freeze for 30 minutes.

For the vanilla layer, stir the condensed milk and coconut butter in a saucepan over a medium–low heat without boiling until melted. Remove from the heat and add the white chocolate and vanilla extract. Mix well until the chocolate is melted. Working quickly, evenly spoon the mixture on top of the strawberry layer, smoothing the top. Freeze for 2 hours to set.

Remove from the tin and discard the baking paper. Cut the fudge into pieces.

Store the fudge in an airtight container in the freezer for up to 1 month.

Makes 12 pieces

CHOCOLATE LAYER
55 g (2 oz) coconut condensed milk
25 g (1 oz) coconut sugar
25 ml (¾ fl oz) maple syrup
50 g (1¾ oz) coconut butter
50 g (1¾ oz) vegan milk chocolate,
  roughly chopped

STRAWBERRY LAYER
100 g (3½ oz) fresh strawberries,
  hulled
55 g (2 oz) coconut condensed milk
25 g (1 oz) coconut sugar
2 teaspoons maple syrup
50 g (1¾ oz) coconut butter
60 g (2 oz) vegan white chocolate,
  roughly chopped (see note)

VANILLA LAYER
105 g (3½ oz/⅓ cup) coconut
  condensed milk
60 g (2 oz) coconut butter
50 g (1¾ oz) vegan white
  chocolate, roughly chopped
  (see note)
1 teaspoon vanilla extract

NOTE
If you can't find vegan white chocolate you can use raw cacao butter buttons.

PEANUT BERRYBUTTER FUDGE

DAIRY FREE, GLUTEN FREE, VEGAN

Line the base and sides of a 10.5 cm × 20 cm (4¼ in × 8 in) loaf (bar) tin with baking paper, ensuring the paper hangs over the sides of the tin for easy removal.

For the peanut layer, put the condensed milk, sugar, maple syrup, peanut butter and coconut butter in a saucepan over a medium–low heat. Cook, stirring, without boiling for 5 minutes or until the sugar has dissolved. Remove from the heat and add the white chocolate, mixing well until the chocolate is melted. Working quickly, spoon the mixture into the prepared loaf tin and smooth the top. Freeze for 30 minutes.

For the berry layer, purée the raspberries in a high-speed blender. Strain the purée through a fine-mesh sieve, reserving the liquid. Discard (or save for later and eat) the pulp and put the liquid, condensed milk and coconut butter in a saucepan over a medium–low heat.

Cook, stirring, without boiling until the coconut butter has melted. Remove from the heat and add the white chocolate, mixing well until the chocolate is melted. Working quickly, evenly spoon the mixture into the prepared tin and spread on top of the peanut layer, smoothing the top. Freeze for 2 hours to set.

Remove from the tin and discard the baking paper. Cut the fudge into pieces.

Store in an airtight container in the freezer for up to 1 month.

Makes 12 pieces

PEANUT LAYER
80 g (2¾ oz/¼ cup) coconut condensed milk
35 g (1¼ oz) coconut sugar (see note)
35 ml (1¼ fl oz) maple syrup
50 g (1¾ oz) peanut butter (see note)
55 g (2 oz) coconut butter
70 g (2½ oz) vegan white chocolate, roughly chopped (see note)

BERRY LAYER
100 g (3½ oz) fresh raspberries
80 g (2¾ oz/¼ cup) coconut condensed milk
100 g (3½ oz) coconut butter
120 g (4½ oz) vegan white chocolate, roughly chopped (see note)

NOTES
You can replace the coconut sugar with rapadura sugar and the maple syrup with rice malt syrup.

You can replace the peanut butter with tahini, sunflower kernel butter or any nut or seed butter of choice!

You can replace the vegan white chocolate with raw cacao butter buttons.

JERSEY CARAMELS

DAIRY FREE, GLUTEN FREE, VEGAN

This one's for Mum. When we were growing up, jersey caramels were our favourite movie treat. We'd always finish the bag before the credits rolled.

Line the base and sides of a 17 cm × 17 cm (6¾ in × 6¾ in) cake tin with baking paper, ensuring the paper hangs over the sides of the tin for easy removal.

For the first caramel layer, put half the condensed milk, half the sugar, half the maple syrup and half the cashew nut butter in a saucepan over a medium–low heat. Cook, stirring, without boiling for 5 minutes or until the sugar has dissolved. Remove from the heat and add half the white chocolate and mix well, ensuring the chocolate is melted. Working quickly, spoon the mixture into the prepared tin and smooth the top. Freeze for 30 minutes.

For the cream layer, melt the coconut butter, cashew nut butter and maple syrup in a saucepan over a medium–low heat until it's smooth and combined. Remove from the heat and add the vanilla extract. Evenly spread the cream on top of the caramel layer, smoothing the top, then freeze for 1 hour to set. This layer needs to be completely set before you add the top caramel layer.

For the top caramel layer, heat the remaining condensed milk, sugar, maple syrup and cashew nut butter in a saucepan over a medium–low heat. Cook, stirring, without boiling for 5 minutes or until the sugar has dissolved.

Remove from the heat and add the remaining white chocolate, mixing well and ensuring the chocolate is melted. Working quickly, spread the mixture evenly on top of the cream layer, smoothing the top. Return the tin to the freezer for 2 hours.

Slice into small cubes.

Store in an airtight container in the freezer for up to 1 month.

Makes 48 caramels

CARAMEL LAYERS
160 g (5½ oz/½ cup) coconut condensed milk
70 g (2½ oz) coconut sugar
70 ml (2¼ fl oz) maple syrup
150 g (5½ oz) cashew nut butter
140 g (5 oz) vegan white chocolate, roughly chopped

CREAM LAYER
100 g (3½ oz) coconut butter
70 g (2½ oz) cashew nut butter
30 ml (1 fl oz) maple syrup
½ teaspoon vanilla extract

SLICES
AND BARS

TRIPLE LAYER CARAMEL CREAM

DAIRY FREE, GLUTEN FREE, VEGAN

Line the base and sides of a 17 cm × 17 cm (6¾ in × 6¾ in) cake tin with baking paper, ensuring the paper hangs over the sides of the tin for easy removal.

Combine all the base ingredients in a food processor until a dough has formed. Press evenly into the prepared cake tin, and freeze while you prepare the remaining layers.

For the cream layer, put the cashew nuts in a bowl and cover with boiling water. Set aside to soak for 30 minutes. Drain and rinse very well.

Blend the drained cashew nuts in a food processor or high-speed blender with the coconut, vanilla extract, milk, coconut oil and rice malt syrup until smooth and creamy. Spread over the base layer and freeze for 30 minutes.

For the caramel layer, carefully blend the dates, salt and water in a food processor until smooth.

Spread the caramel layer onto the cream layer. Freeze for 1 hour.

Remove from the tin, cut into slices and serve.

Store the remaining slices in an airtight container in the fridge for up to 1 week or in the freezer for up to 1 month.

Makes 18 slices

BASE
60 g (2 oz/½ cup) cacao powder
90 ml (3 fl oz) rice malt syrup
200 g (7 oz) raw walnuts

CREAM LAYER
230 g (8 oz) dry-roasted unsalted
  cashew nuts
50 g (1¾ oz) unsweetened
  desiccated coconut
½ teaspoon vanilla extract
80 ml (2½ fl oz/⅓ cup) plant-
  based milk
45 g (1½ fl oz) coconut oil
70 ml (2¼ fl oz) rice malt syrup

CARAMEL LAYER
260 g (9 oz) soft medjool dates,
  pitted
¼ teaspoon ground sea salt
40 ml (1¼ fl oz) boiling water

CHRISTMAS PUDDING SLICE

DAIRY FREE, GLUTEN FREE, VEGAN

All the goodness of Christmas pudding, jam-packed into a hedgehog slice – rum included.

In a small bowl combine the raisins and rum, then leave to soak for 30 minutes.

Line the base and sides of a 17 cm × 17 cm (6¾ in × 6¾ in) cake tin with baking paper, ensuring the paper hangs over the sides of the tin for easy removal.

In a food processor pulse the arrowroot biscuits until slightly crushed. Transfer to a large bowl.

Add the coconut, cacao powder, apricots, cranberries, orange zest and soaked raisins. Mix to combine.

In a saucepan over a medium–low heat, mix the almond butter, rice malt syrup and coconut oil until melted and smooth. Remove from the heat and add to the dry ingredients. Mix well.

Press the mixture into the prepared cake tin. Freeze for 1 hour or until firm.

Remove from the tin, slice into squares and serve.

Store the remaining slices in an airtight container in the freezer for up to 1 month.

Makes 16 slices

100 g (3½ oz) raisins
50 ml (1¾ fl oz) sweet rum
200 g (7 oz) gluten-free, vegan arrowroot biscuits
40 g (1½ oz) unsweetened desiccated coconut
40 g (1½ oz/⅓ cup) cacao powder
100 g (3½ oz) dried apricots, roughly chopped
100 g (3½ oz) dried cranberries
1 tablespoon finely grated orange zest
135 g (4¾ oz) almond butter (see note)
90 ml (3 fl oz) rice malt syrup
40 g (1½ oz) coconut oil

NOTE
You can replace the almond butter with a seed butter of choice to make this recipe nut free.

CHERRY SQUARES

DAIRY FREE, GLUTEN FREE, NUT FREE, VEGAN

Line a 38 cm × 25 cm (15 in × 10 in) baking tray (cookie sheet) with baking paper. Line the base and sides of a 30 cm × 20 cm × 3.5 cm deep (12 in × 8 in × 1½ in) slice tin.

For the cherry layer, thoroughly mix all the ingredients in a large bowl, then pour into the prepared slice tin. Freeze for 1 hour. Remove from the freezer, then use a warm, sharp knife to cut into twenty-two squares.

For the chocolate layer, add 5 cm (2 in) water to a large saucepan and bring to the boil over a medium–high heat. Set a medium glass or ceramic mixing bowl on top of the saucepan, making sure the mixing bowl isn't touching the water. Add the cacao buttons to the mixing bowl and melt for about 3 minutes. Once melted, whisk in the maple syrup until combined.

Turn off the heat, remove the bowl and set on a flat surface. Whisk the cacao powder and vanilla extract into the melted cacao butter mixture until smooth. Set aside for 2 minutes to cool and thicken slightly.

One by one, dip the cherry squares into the chocolate and shake the bowl slightly to coat. Remove the squares with a fork and place on the prepared baking tray. Refrigerate for 30 minutes.

Store in an airtight container in the fridge for 1 week or in the freezer for up to 1 month.

Makes 22 squares

CHERRY CENTRE

320 g (11½ oz/3½ cups) desiccated coconut
320 g (11½ oz/1 cup) condensed coconut milk
150 g (5½ oz) dried cherries, chopped
200 g (7 oz) frozen cherries, thawed
½ teaspoon vanilla extract
1 teaspoon raspberry powder

CHOCOLATE

200 g (7 oz) cacao butter buttons
85 ml (2¾ fl oz) pure maple syrup
50 g (1¾ oz) cacao powder
1 teaspoon vanilla extract

PEPPERMINT SLICE

DAIRY FREE, GLUTEN FREE, VEGAN

Forget after-dinner mints. This cheesecake is every bit as creamy and refreshing. A welcome treat after any meal.

Put the cashew nuts for the filling in a large bowl and cover with boiling water. Soak for 30 minutes.

Line the base and sides of a 20 cm × 20 cm × 7 cm deep (8 in × 8 in × 2¾ in) springform cake tin with baking paper.

Blend the base ingredients and 30 ml (1 fl oz) water in a food processor until the mixture starts to come together. Press the mixture firmly into the base of the prepared tin. Put it in the freezer while you prepare the filling.

Drain and rinse the cashew nuts very well. Blend the drained cashew nuts, rice malt syrup, coconut oil, coconut cream, mint leaves and lemon juice in a food processor until smooth and well combined. Add the peppermint extract and spirulina and blend to combine. Pour the mixture over the base and freeze for 3 hours to set.

To serve, remove the slice from the freezer and set aside at room temperature for 30 minutes. Using a warm, sharp knife, cut into slices.

For the topping, in a bowl mix the rice malt syrup, coconut oil, cacao powder and vanilla extract until smooth. Using a piping (icing) bag or spoon, drizzle the mixture over the squares.

Store the remaining slices in an airtight container in the freezer for up to 1 month.

Makes 18 slices

BASE

70 g (2½ oz) medjool dates, pitted
40 ml (1¼ fl oz) rice malt syrup
  (see note)
30 g (1 oz) unsweetened desiccated
  coconut
300 g (10½ oz) raw almonds
25 g (1 oz) cacao powder

FILLING

300 g (10½ oz) raw cashew nuts
180 ml (6 fl oz) rice malt syrup
  (see note)
60 g (2 oz) coconut oil
400 ml (13½ fl oz) tinned coconut
  cream
5 g (¼ oz/¼ cup) fresh mint
  leaves
60 ml (2 fl oz/¼ cup) lemon juice
2 teaspoons peppermint extract
¼ teaspoon spirulina

TOPPING

35 ml (1¼ fl oz) rice malt syrup
  (see note)
35 g (1¼ oz) coconut oil, melted
25 g (1 oz) cacao powder
1 teaspoon vanilla extract

NOTE
You can use maple syrup
in place of rice malt syrup.

MARZ BAR

DAIRY FREE, GLUTEN FREE, VEGAN

Line a baking tray and the base and sides of a 30 cm × 20 cm × 3.5 cm deep (12 in × 8 in × 1½ in) slice tin with baking paper.

For the nougat base, melt the cashew butter, coconut butter and maple syrup in a medium saucepan over a medium–low heat until smooth. Remove from the heat and stir through the coconut flour, salt and vanilla extract until a dough-like mixture forms.

Press the mixture evenly into the prepared slice tin. Freeze while you make the caramel.

For the caramel, combine all the ingredients in a high-speed blender or food processor until smooth. Spread the caramel over the base layer, then return the tin to the freezer for 15 minutes. Remove from the freezer and cut into bars.

For the chocolate layer, add 5 cm (2 in) water to a large saucepan and bring to the boil over a medium–high heat. Set a medium glass or ceramic mixing bowl on top, making sure the mixing bowl isn't touching the water. Add the cacao buttons to the mixing bowl and melt for about 3 minutes. Once melted, whisk in the maple syrup until combined. Turn off the heat, remove the bowl and set on a flat surface.

Whisk the cacao powder and vanilla extract into the melted cacao butter mixture until smooth. Set aside for 2 minutes to cool and thicken slightly.

Using two forks, dip the bars into the chocolate and place on the prepared baking tray. Refrigerate for 30 minutes.

Store in an airtight container in the fridge for 1 week or in the freezer for up to 1 month.

Makes 12 large bars

NOUGAT BASE

200 g (7 oz) cashew butter
80 g (2¾ oz) coconut butter
100 ml (3½ fl oz) maple syrup
80 g (2¾ oz) coconut flour
¼ teaspoon sea salt
½ teaspoon vanilla extract

CARAMEL

350 g (12½ oz) medjool dates, pitted
60 ml (2 fl oz/¼ cup) coconut milk
1 tablespoon hulled tahini
¼ teaspoon sea salt
½ teaspoon vanilla extract

CHOCOLATE

200 g (7 oz) cacao butter buttons
85 ml (2¾ fl oz) pure maple syrup
50 g (1¾ oz) cacao powder, sifted
1 teaspoon vanilla extract

CHOCOLATE BROWNIES

DAIRY FREE, GLUTEN FREE, VEGAN

Preheat the oven to 180°C (160°C fan forced/350°F). Line the base and sides of a 26 cm × 16.5 cm (10¼ in × 6½ in) slice tin with baking paper, allowing the sides to overhang.

Drain the chickpeas, reserving 60 ml (2 fl oz/¼ cup) chickpea water (aquafaba) in a bowl. Transfer the chickpeas to a container and refrigerate for another use.

In a small bowl thoroughly mix the chia seeds and 85 ml (2¾ fl oz) water. Set aside to become gelatinous.

In a large bowl, mix the aquafaba, chia mixture, cacao powder, stevia, baking powder, coffee, salt and vanilla extract until combined. Set aside.

Put the coconut oil, sugar and apple sauce in a saucepan over a medium heat. Cook, constantly stirring until melted and barely bubbling.

Add the hot coconut oil mixture to the chocolate mixture and stir until well combined.

Add the flour and mix to form a thick batter. The mixture will remain slightly lumpy. Allow the batter to rest for 20 minutes.

After resting, gently stir in the chocolate, then pour the mixture into the prepared tin. Use a spatula to smooth the batter evenly into the corners of the pan.

Bake for 30 minutes. A toothpick inserted into the centre should reveal very moist crumbs. Before removing from the pan, allow to cool completely on a wire rack.

Slice and garnish the brownies with a sprinkling of chopped hazelnuts.

Store any leftover brownies in an airtight container in the fridge for up to 1 week.

Makes 12 large brownies

400 g (14 oz) tin salt-free chickpeas
25 g (1 oz) chia seeds
100 g (3½ oz) cacao powder
1 teaspoon green leaf stevia
1 teaspoon baking powder
½ teaspoon finely ground coffee
1 teaspoon ground sea salt
20 ml (¾ fl oz) vanilla extract
100 g (3½ oz) coconut oil
180 g (6½ oz) rapadura sugar
125 g (4½ oz) unsweetened apple sauce
180 g (6½ oz) gluten-free plain (all-purpose) flour
125 g (4½ oz) vegan milk chocolate, roughly chopped
dry-roasted unsalted hazelnuts, roughly chopped, to garnish

DATE CRUMBLE SLICE

DAIRY FREE, GLUTEN FREE, VEGAN

Preheat the oven to 180°C (160°C fan forced/350°F). Line the base and sides of a 17 cm × 17 cm (6¾ in × 6¾ in) cake tin with baking paper, ensuring the paper hangs over the sides of the tin for easy removal.

Combine the dates, maple syrup and 120 ml (4 fl oz) water in a medium saucepan over a medium–high heat. Bring to the boil, stirring frequently, for about 3 minutes or until the dates are pulpy. Remove from heat, stir in the orange juice and set aside to cool.

Pulse the walnuts in a food processor until a flour forms. Set aside in a large bowl.

Blend the coconut milk, vanilla extract and sugar in a food processor until combined. Add the flour, sea salt, cinnamon, bicarbonate of soda and walnut flour. Process until a dough forms, being careful not to overmix.

Evenly press three-quarters of the dough into the base of the prepared pan. Spread the date mixture over the top.

Crumble the remaining dough mixture over the date mixture so the dates are completely covered, pressing the dough gently into the date mixture with your fingertips.

Bake for 30–35 minutes, or until golden. Allow to cool completely in the tin.

Remove from the tin and slice.

Store in an airtight container in the fridge for up to 1 week.

Makes 6 large slices or 12 small slices

320 g (11 ½ oz) dried dates, pitted and roughly chopped
50 ml (1¾ fl oz) maple syrup
80 ml (2½ fl oz/⅓ cup) freshly squeezed orange juice
165 g (6 oz) raw walnuts (see note)
145 ml (5 fl oz) tinned coconut milk
1 teaspoon vanilla extract
80 g (2¾ oz) coconut sugar
345 g (12 oz) gluten-free plain (all-purpose) flour
¼ teaspoon ground sea salt
1 teaspoon ground cinnamon
½ teaspoon bicarbonate of soda (baking soda)

NOTE
You can replace the walnuts with gluten-free oats to make this recipe nut free.

CHOC CARAMEL SLICE

DAIRY FREE, GLUTEN FREE, VEGAN

Oozy, gooey and full of sticky goodness, this slice is for the fussy eaters who criticise allergy-friendly treats. Prepare to be converted.

Line the base and sides of a 17 cm × 17 cm (6¾ in × 6¾ in) cake tin with baking paper, ensuring the paper hangs over the sides of the tin for easy removal.

Blend all the base ingredients and 30 ml (1 fl oz) water in a food processor until a dough forms and the mixture sticks together when pressed. Add more water if the mixture is too dry.

Using a wet spoon, press the base mixture evenly into the prepared tin and freeze for 30 minutes.

Blend all the caramel ingredients in a high-speed blender or food processor until smooth. The mixture will look a little split. Transfer to a small saucepan over a medium–low heat and cook until the mixture comes together and forms a smooth, thick caramel. Spread the caramel on top of the base. Freeze for 30 minutes.

Mix all the chocolate ingredients in a bowl until smooth. Spread on top of the caramel. Freeze for 2 hours.

Remove from the tin, slice and serve.

Store in an airtight container in the fridge for 1 week or in the freezer for up to 1 month.

Makes 16 large slices or 32 small slices

BASE
230 g (8 oz) raw cashew nuts
40 g (1½ oz) desiccated coconut
115 g (4 oz) soft medjool dates, pitted
1 teaspoon ground cinnamon

CARAMEL
40 g (1½ oz) tinned coconut cream
200 g (7 oz) soft medjool dates, pitted
150 g (5½ oz) hulled tahini
30 g (1 oz) coconut oil, melted
1 teaspoon vanilla extract
¼ teaspoon ground sea salt

CHOCOLATE (SEE NOTE)
55 g (2 oz) cacao powder
100 g (3½ oz) coconut oil, melted
85 ml (2¾ fl oz) maple syrup

NOTE
You can use 130 g (4½ oz) of vegan milk chocolate to melt on top instead of making your own.

STRAWBERRY BLONDE BARS

DAIRY FREE, GLUTEN FREE, VEGAN

Put the cashew nuts for the filling in a large bowl and cover with boiling water. Soak for 30 minutes.

Line the base and sides of a 20 cm × 20 cm × 7 cm deep (8 in × 8 in × 2¾ in) springform cake tin with baking paper, allowing the sides to overhang. Set aside.

Blend the base ingredients and 30 ml (1 fl oz) water in a food processor until the mixture starts to come together. Press the mixture firmly into the base of the prepared tin. Freeze while you prepare the filling.

Drain and rinse the cashew nuts very well. Blend the cashew nuts, rice malt syrup, coconut oil, coconut cream, lemon juice and vanilla extract in a food processor until silky smooth and well combined.

Remove half the filling from the food processor and set aside. Add the strawberries to the food processor and blend until smooth. Pour the strawberry filling over the base and freeze for 1½ hours.

Once set, pour the remaining filling over the strawberry layer. Freeze for 1 hour.

Before serving, sit at room temperature for 30 minutes. Carefully remove from the cake tin and discard the baking paper.

Cut into bars using a warm, sharp knife. Garnish each bar with a drizzle of melted coconut butter and chopped macadamia nuts. Decorate with a halved strawberry to serve.

Store the remaining bars in an airtight container in the freezer for up to 1 month.

Makes 18 bars

BASE

80 g (2¾ oz) medjool dates, pitted
80 ml (2½ fl oz/⅓ cup) rice malt syrup (see note)
50 g (1¾ oz) unsweetened desiccated coconut
170 g (6 oz) raw macadamia nuts
170 g (6 oz) buckwheat kernels

FILLING

300 g (10½ oz) raw cashew nuts
180 ml (6 fl oz) rice malt syrup (see note)
60 g (2 oz) coconut oil
400 ml (13½ fl oz) tinned coconut cream
60 ml (2 fl oz/¼ cup) freshly squeezed lemon juice
1 teaspoon vanilla extract
180 g (6½ oz) fresh strawberries, hulled

GARNISH

100 g (3½ oz) coconut butter, melted
9 fresh strawberries, halved
20 g (¾ oz) macadamia nuts, chopped

NOTES
You can use maple syrup in place of rice malt syrup.

MUESLI SLICE

DAIRY FREE, GLUTEN FREE, VEGAN

Line the base and sides of a 20 cm × 20 cm × 7 cm deep (8 in × 8 in × 2¾ in) springform cake tin with baking paper, allowing the sides to overhang. Set aside.

Blend all the base ingredients in a food processor until the dough starts to stick together.

Using the back of a spoon, firmly press the base mixture evenly into the prepared tin. Freeze for 30 minutes.

Combine the pepitas, pecans, macadamia nuts, sesame seeds, cranberries, apricots and figs in a bowl. Mix well.

In a small saucepan over a low heat, melt the maple syrup, tahini, coconut butter, coconut sugar and cinnamon until combined. Remove from the heat, add the vanilla extract and mix well. Pour over the nut mixture and, using a strong arm, mix well.

Spread over the base, creating an even layer. Freeze for 1 hour.

Cut into slices, then dip each slice into the melted white chocolate and place on baking paper until set.

Serve and enjoy.

Store the remaining slices in an airtight container in the freezer for up to 1 month.

Makes 24 small slices

BASE

30 ml (1 fl oz) orange juice
1 tablespoon orange zest
145 g (5 oz) desiccated coconut
130 g (4½ oz) raw buckwheat kernels
130 g (4½ oz) soft medjool dates, pitted
40 g (1½ oz) cashew nut butter

TOPPING

80 g (2¾ oz) pepitas (pumpkin seeds)
80 g (2¾ oz) pecans, roughly chopped
80 g (2¾ oz) macadamia nuts, roughly chopped
1 tablespoon sesame seeds
80 g (2¾ oz) dried cranberries
80 g (2¾ oz) dried apricots, roughly chopped
80 g (2¾ oz) dried figs, finely sliced
100 ml (3½ fl oz) maple syrup
120 g (4½ oz) hulled tahini
60 g (2 oz) coconut butter
20 g (¾ oz) coconut sugar
1 teaspoon ground cinnamon
1 teaspoon vanilla extract
80 g (2¾ oz) vegan white chocolate, melted (see note)

NOTE
You can use melted coconut butter in place of white chocolate.

CHOCKETO BARS

DAIRY FREE, GLUTEN FREE, VEGAN

Line the base and sides of a 23 cm x 23 cm (9 in x 9 in) cake tin with baking paper, ensuring the paper hangs over the sides of the tin for easy removal. Line a 38 cm × 25 cm (15 in × 10 in) baking tray (cookie sheet) with baking paper.

For the caramel fudge, heat the condensed milk, coconut sugar and cashew nut butter in a saucepan over a medium–low heat. Stir without boiling for 10 minutes or until the sugar has dissolved and the cashew nut butter has melted. Add the cacao butter buttons and vanilla extract and stir until melted. Remove from the heat and, working quickly, spoon the mixture into the prepared tin, smoothing the top. Lightly press half the puffed rice over the top of the caramel to create an even layer. Freeze for 2 hours.

Once set, remove from the freezer and cut into bars using a warm, sharp knife. Lightly press the sides of each bar with the remaining rice puffs to create an even coating. Return to the freezer while you make the chocolate.

For the chocolate, add 5 cm (2 in) water to a large saucepan and bring to the boil over a medium–high heat. Set a medium glass or ceramic mixing bowl on top, making sure the mixing bowl isn't touching the water. Add the cacao buttons to the mixing bowl and melt for about 3 minutes. Once melted, whisk in the maple syrup until combined. Turn off the heat, remove the bowl and set on a flat surface.

Add the cacao powder and vanilla extract and whisk until smooth.

One by one, dip each bar into the chocolate and shake the bowl slightly to coat. Remove the bars with a fork and place on the prepared baking tray. Refrigerate for 30 minutes.

Store in an airtight container in the fridge for 1 week or in the freezer for up to 1 month.

Makes 16 large bars

60 g (2 oz) puffed rice

CARAMEL FUDGE
320 g (11½ oz) condensed coconut milk
140 g (5 oz) coconut sugar
250 g (9 oz) cashew nut butter
230 g (8 oz) cacao butter buttons
1 teaspoon vanilla extract

CHOCOLATE
200 g (7 oz) cacao butter buttons
85 ml (2¾ fl oz) pure maple syrup
50 g (1¾ oz) cacao powder
1 teaspoon vanilla extract

CAKES AND
CHEESECAKES

DOUBLE-CHOCOLATE CUPCAKES

DAIRY FREE, GLUTEN FREE, NUT FREE, VEGAN

Preheat the oven to 175°C (155°C fan forced/350°F). Line a twelve-hole standard muffin tin with silicone cupcake liners.

In a small bowl, thoroughly mix the chia seeds and 30 ml (1 fl oz) water. Set aside to become gelatinous.

Whisk sugar, flour, cacao powder, baking powder, bicarbonate of soda and salt in a large bowl to combine. Mix coconut cream, apple sauce, vanilla extract, boiling water and chia mixture in a separate bowl. Add the wet ingredients to the dry and mix until just combined. Divide the mixture evenly into the prepared silicone liners until they are three-quarters full.

Bake for 30–40 minutes or until a skewer inserted in the centre of a cupcake comes out with a few moist crumbs attached.

Stand the cupcakes in the tin for 5 minutes before turning them out onto a wire rack to cool completely, top-side up.

Once cool, cut a deep circle into the top of each cupcake using the bottom of a small piping tip. Reserve the cut-outs for a chef's snack.

To make the caramel, blend the dates and sea salt in a food processor until small pieces remain. Slowly add 60 ml (2 fl oz/¼ cup) water until a thick caramel has formed. Set aside 70 g of the caramel for icing (frosting). Use the remaining caramel to fill the hole in each cupcake.

For the icing, mix all the ingredients in a high-speed blender or food processor until smooth and thick. Transfer the icing to a large bowl, cover with plastic wrap and refrigerate for 30 minutes to set.

Prepare a large piping (icing) bag with a closed-star tip. Fill the bag with icing and pipe onto the cupcakes.

The cupcakes can be stored in an airtight container in the fridge for 1 week.

Makes 12

CAKE
2 teaspoons chia seeds
110 g (4 oz) rapadura sugar
135 g (5 oz) gluten-free plain (all-purpose) flour
45 g (1½ oz) cacao powder
¾ teaspoon baking powder
¾ teaspoon bicarbonate of soda (baking soda)
½ teaspoon ground sea salt
90 ml (3 fl oz) coconut cream
80 g (2¾ oz) apple sauce
3 teaspoons vanilla extract
125 ml (4 fl oz/½ cup) boiling water

CARAMEL
210 g (7½ oz) soft medjool dates, pitted and roughly chopped
¼ teaspoon ground sea salt

ICING / FROSTING
50 g (1¾ oz) rapadura sugar
210 g (7½ oz) orange sweet potato purée (see note)
50 g (1¾ oz) cacao powder
15 g (½ oz) arrowroot starch
1 teaspoon vanilla extract
70 g (2½ oz) reserved caramel
20 g (¾ oz) coconut butter, melted

NOTE
For the orange sweet potato purée, steam or boil peeled orange sweet potato until tender. Drain and mash until a thick purée forms.

CAPPUCCINO CAKES

DAIRY FREE, GLUTEN FREE, VEGAN

When you need a sweet little kicker, these are made with real coffee to give you a shot in the arm.

Preheat the oven to 175°C (155°C fan forced/350°F). Line a twelve-hole standard muffin tin with silicone cupcake liners.

In a small bowl, thoroughly mix the chia seeds and 115 ml (4 fl oz) water. Set aside to become gelatinous.

Pour the boiling water over the coffee granules and mix well. Set aside to cool to room temperature.

In a large bowl whisk the flour, sugar, salt and bicarbonate of soda to combine.

In a separate bowl, whisk the melted coconut oil, vanilla extract, coconut cream, chia mixture and cooled coffee mixture to combine.

Add the wet ingredients to the dry and mix until just combined.

Divide the mixture evenly into the prepared silicone liners, filling each liner to the top.

Bake for 35–40 minutes or until a skewer inserted into the centre of a cupcake comes out clean. Stand the cupcakes in the tin for 5 minutes before turning them out onto a wire rack to cool completely, top-side up.

Bake the remaining cupcake mixture (it should make two more cupcakes).

For the icing (frosting), mix all the ingredients in a high-speed blender or food processor until the icing is smooth and thick. Transfer to a large bowl, cover with plastic wrap and freeze for 30 minutes to set.

Ice each cupcake with a thick layer of icing and a sprinkle of grated white chocolate.

Serve and enjoy!

Store the remaining cupcakes in an airtight container in the fridge for 1 week.

Makes 14

50 g (1¾ oz) vegan white chocolate, grated, to garnish

CAKE
30 g (1 oz) chia seeds
130 ml (4½ fl oz) boiling water
15 g (½ oz) instant coffee granules
420 g (15 oz) gluten-free plain (all-purpose) flour
150 g (5½ oz) rapadura sugar
¾ teaspoon ground sea salt
1½ teaspoons bicarbonate of soda (baking soda)
80 ml (2½ fl oz/⅓ cup) coconut oil, melted
3 teaspoons vanilla extract
300 ml (10 fl oz) tinned coconut cream

ICING / FROSTING
400 g (14 oz) white sweet potato purée (see note)
20 ml (¾ fl oz) espresso
1 teaspoon vanilla extract
100 g (3½ oz) rapadura sugar
3 teaspoons arrowroot starch
60 g (2 oz) cashew nut butter
30 ml (1 fl oz) milk

NOTE
For the white sweet potato purée, steam or boil peeled sweet potato until tender. Drain and mash until a thick purée forms.

LEMON MERINGUE CUPCAKES

DAIRY FREE, GLUTEN FREE, NUT FREE, VEGAN

Preheat the oven to 170°C (150°C fan forced/340°F). Line a twelve-hole standard muffin tin with silicone cupcake liners.

In a large bowl, sift the flour, baking powder, cornflour, sugar and sea salt together. In a separate bowl mix the rice milk, apple sauce, vanilla extract, lemon juice and lemon zest. Add the wet mixture to the dry and fold through until just incorporated. Fill the cupcake liners until they are three-quarters full.

Bake for 40–45 minutes or until a skewer inserted into a cupcake comes out clean. Stand for 5 minutes before turning them out onto a wire rack to cool, top-side up.

To make the lemon curd, combine all the ingredients in a small saucepan over a medium–high heat. Whisk continuously for 5–7 minutes or until the mixture is smooth and thickened. Remove from the heat and allow it to cool completely.

Cut a deep hole in the top of each cooled cupcake with a small piping tip. Be careful not to cut through to the bottom of the cupcake. Fill each hole with lemon curd.

For the meringue, drain the chickpeas and reserve 145 ml (5 fl oz) chilled chickpea water (aquafaba) in a large glass or metal mixing bowl. You want the bowl to be completely clean and free of grease. You can use lemon juice to clean the bowl and rinse before use.

Using an electric mixer with a whisk attachment, whisk the chickpea aquafaba and cream of tartar on medium speed until stiff peaks form. Continue mixing and add the sugar one tablespoon at a time until it's incorporated. Once all the sugar is added continue whisking for a further minute. Add the vanilla extract and whisk for another 30 seconds.

Spoon the meringue into a piping (icing) bag with a large star-shaped nozzle and pipe it onto the cupcakes. Place under a preheated grill (broiler) until lightly golden, or use a small blowtorch to brown them.

Serve immediately and enjoy!

Makes 12

CAKE
200 g (7 oz) gluten-free plain (all-purpose) flour
2 teaspoons baking powder
2 tablespoons cornflour (cornstarch)
150 g (5½ oz) rapadura sugar
½ teaspoon ground sea salt
250 ml (8½ fl oz/1 cup) rice milk, room temperature
80 g (2¾ oz) unsweetened apple sauce
2 teaspoons vanilla extract
2 tablespoons lemon juice
1 teaspoon finely grated lemon zest

LEMON CURD
125 ml (4 fl oz/½ cup) lemon juice
1 teaspoon finely grated lemon zest
30 ml (1 fl oz) tinned coconut milk
1 tablespoon cornflour (cornstarch)
¼ teaspoon turmeric
60 ml (2 fl oz/¼ cup) maple syrup

MERINGUE
400 g (14 oz) tin salt-free chickpeas, chilled overnight
½ teaspoon cream of tartar
145 g (5 oz) caster (superfine) sugar (see note)
½ teaspoon vanilla extract

NOTE
You can substitute the caster sugar in the meringue with 145 g (5 oz) rapadura sugar mixed with 1 teaspoon of arrowroot starch. It will still work, but it will produce a flatter meringue with a less airy texture.

RED VELVET CAKE

DAIRY FREE, GLUTEN FREE, NUT FREE, VEGAN

Red velvet will always hold a special place in my heart. This was the flavour and inspiration for my wedding cake. My creation uses beetroot (beet) powder and raspberry purée, which add a rich, natural food colouring.

Line the base and sides of two 20 cm wide × 7 cm deep (8 in × 2¾ in) round springform cake tins with baking paper. Preheat the oven to 180°C (160°C fan forced/350°F).

Mix the milk and apple cider vinegar in a small bowl. Set aside for 10 minutes.

Sift the flour, sugar, cacao powder, baking powder, cream of tartar and salt into a large bowl.

To the milk mixture add the melted coconut oil, raspberry purée, apple sauce, lemon juice, beetroot powder and vanilla extract. Mix well. Add the wet mixture to the dry and mix to combine. Evenly distribute the batter into the prepared cake tins.

Bake for 25–35 minutes or until a skewer inserted into the centre of the cakes comes out clean.

Let the cakes cool in the tins for 10 minutes before turning out onto a wire rack to cool completely.

For the icing (frosting), mix all the ingredients in a high-speed blender or food processor until the icing is smooth and thick. If the icing is too runny, place it in the fridge to thicken for 15 minutes.

Sandwich the two cakes together using a third of the icing between the layers. Smooth the remaining icing over the entire cake and garnish with fresh strawberries.

Slice and serve!

The cake can be stored in an airtight container in the fridge for up to 3 days or sliced, wrapped in plastic wrap and frozen for up to 1 month.

Serves 12

100 g (3½ oz) fresh strawberries to garnish

CAKE

180 ml (6 fl oz) plant-based milk
30 ml (1 fl oz) apple cider vinegar
400 g (14 oz) gluten-free plain (all-purpose) flour
280 g (10 oz) rapadura sugar
1 tablespoon cacao powder
2 teaspoons baking powder
1 teaspoon cream of tartar
1 teaspoon ground sea salt
100 g (3½ oz) coconut oil, melted
240 g (8½ oz) frozen raspberries, warmed and mashed to a purée
110 g (4 oz) unsweetened apple sauce
40 ml (1¼ fl oz) lemon juice
40 g (1½ oz) beetroot (beet) powder (see note)
1 tablespoon vanilla extract

ICING / FROSTING

130 g (5 oz) vegan white chocolate, melted
50 g (1¾ oz) coconut butter, melted
200 ml (7 fl oz) coconut cream
200 g (7 oz) desiccated coconut
1 tablespoon arrowroot starch
1 teaspoon vanilla extract

NOTE
You can substitute 100 g (3½ oz) raw beetroot purée for the beetroot powder. If you take this option, you will have to reduce the raspberry purée to 140 g (5 oz) from 240 g (8½ oz).

TRIPLE-CHOC MUDCAKE

DAIRY FREE, GLUTEN FREE, NUT FREE, VEGAN

Line the base and sides of two 20 cm wide × 7 cm deep (8 in × 3 in) round springform cake tins with baking paper. Preheat the oven to 150°C (130°C fan forced/300°F).

In a small bowl, thoroughly mix the chia seeds and 80 ml (2½ fl oz/ ⅓ cup) water and set aside to become gelatinous.

In a large saucepan over a medium–low heat, heat the coconut oil, sugar, sweet potato, chocolate and milk. Heat until all the ingredients are melted and incorporated. Remove from the heat and add the chia mixture and vanilla extract. Mix well and set aside to cool.

In a large bowl, sift flour, cacao powder, baking powder and salt. Add the cooled chocolate mix and stir well.

Divide the mixture between the two prepared cake tins. Bake for 75–90 minutes. When you insert a skewer into the centre of the cakes, it will emerge with crumbs attached. Roll the crumbs from the skewer on your fingertips – if it balls and feels tacky, the cakes are ready.

Let the cakes cool in the tins for 10 minutes before turning out onto a wire rack to cool completely.

For the icing (frosting), mix all the ingredients in a high-speed blender or food processor until smooth and thick.

Once the cakes are cool, place one cake on a serving plate. Top with the frosting, creating a smooth, even layer. Top with the other cake and lightly press to securely position the cake on the frosting.

For the chocolate topping, combine all the ingredients in a bowl until smooth. Drizzle the chocolate over the cake.

Refrigerate for 1 hour to set. Before serving, sift cacao powder over the cake.

Serve and enjoy!

The cake can be stored in an airtight container in the fridge for up to 4 days or sliced, wrapped in cling wrap and frozen for up to 1 month.

Serves 12

CAKE
20 g (¾ oz) chia seeds
100 g (3½ oz) coconut oil
280 g (10 oz) rapadura sugar
150 g (5½ oz) orange sweet potato purée (see note)
200 g (7 oz) vegan milk chocolate
375 ml (12½ fl oz/1½ cups) plant-based milk
3 teaspoons vanilla extract
220 g (8 oz) gluten-free plain (all-purpose) flour
25 g (1 oz) cacao powder
1 teaspoon baking powder
½ teaspoon ground sea salt

ICING / FROSTING FOR FILLING
50 g (1¾ oz) rapadura sugar
250 g (9 oz) orange sweet potato purée (see note)
30 g (1 oz/¼ cup) cacao powder
3 teaspoons arrowroot starch
1 teaspoon vanilla extract
70 ml (2¼ fl oz) maple syrup
60 g (2 oz) vegan milk chocolate, melted

CHOCOLATE TOPPING
20 g (¾ oz) cacao powder, plus extra to garnish
20 ml (¾ fl oz) maple syrup
40 g (1½ oz) coconut oil, melted
½ teaspoon vanilla extract

NOTE
To make the sweet potato purées, steam or boil peeled sweet potato until tender. Drain and mash to a smooth purée.

CHAI CARROT CAKE

DAIRY FREE, GLUTEN FREE, VEGAN

Line the base and sides of two 20 cm (8 in) round springform cake tins with baking paper. Preheat the oven to 180°C (160°C fan forced/350°F).

In a small bowl mix the chia seeds and 125 ml (4 fl oz/½ cup) water. Set aside until thick and gelatinous.

Infuse the chai tea bag in the boiling water for 10 minutes until strong. Discard the tea bag.

In a large bowl, sift the flour, baking powder, bicarbonate of soda, cinnamon, nutmeg, cloves, ginger and sea salt together. Add the grated carrot, sultanas, pistachios, walnuts and coconut and mix thoroughly.

In a separate bowl, beat the chia seed mixture, apple purée, rapadura sugar, coconut milk, maple syrup, vanilla extract and chai tea with an electric mixer until combined. Add the wet mixture to the dry and stir until just combined. Evenly fill the prepared cake tins.

Bake for 1½ hours or until a toothpick inserted into the centre of the cakes comes out clean. Stand the cakes in the tins for 5 minutes before turning them out onto wire racks to cool, top-side up.

For the icing (frosting), put the cashew nuts in a small bowl, cover with boiling water and soak for 30 minutes. Drain and rinse well. Transfer to a high-speed blender or food processor. Add the remaining icing ingredients and blend until smooth. Transfer to a large bowl and refrigerate until ready to use.

For the crumble, add all the ingredients to a small frying pan over a medium–low heat. Toast until the crumble is golden, fragrant and sticky. Set aside to cool.

Sandwich the two cakes together using about one third of the icing. Smooth the remaining icing over the entire cake. Garnish with the crumble. Slice and serve!

The cake can be stored in an airtight container in the fridge for up to 4 days or sliced, wrapped in plastic wrap and frozen for up to 1 month.

Serves 12

CAKE
30 g (1 oz) chia seeds
1 chai tea bag
90 ml (3 fl oz) boiling water
450 g (1 lb) gluten-free plain
  (all-purpose) flour
3 teaspoons baking powder
2 teaspoons bicarbonate of soda
2 teaspoons ground cinnamon
½ teaspoon ground nutmeg
⅛ teaspoon ground cloves
¼ teaspoon ground ginger
½ teaspoon ground sea salt
160 g (5½ oz) grated carrot
90 g (3 oz) sultanas (golden raisins)
80 g (2¾ oz) pistachios, chopped
80 g (2¾ oz) walnuts, chopped
60 g (2 oz) desiccated coconut
230 g (8 oz) apple purée
110 g (4 oz) rapadura sugar
400 ml (13½ fl oz) tinned
  coconut milk
165 ml (5½ fl oz) maple syrup
2 teaspoons vanilla extract

ICING / FROSTING
180 g (6½ oz) raw cashew nuts
100 g (3½ oz) rapadura sugar
2 teaspoons arrowroot powder
220 g (8 oz) orange sweet
  potato purée (see note, page 59)
2 teaspoons finely grated lemon rind
¼ teaspoon ground sea salt
1 teaspoon vanilla extract
1 tablespoon lemon juice
1 tablespoon plant-based milk

CRUMBLE
50 g (1¾ oz) walnuts, chopped
40 g (1½ oz) pistachios, chopped
60 ml (2 fl oz/¼ cup) rice malt syrup
1 teaspoon coconut oil
1 teaspoon cinnamon

DAD'S FRUITCAKE

DAIRY FREE, GLUTEN FREE, VEGAN

Dad would always brag about his fruitcakes, even if they were store bought. We'd enjoy a sneaky slice together for morning or afternoon tea.

Preheat the oven to 180°C (160°C fan forced/350°F). Line the base and sides of a 20 cm (8 in) round springform cake tin with baking paper.

In a saucepan over a medium–low heat, combine the milk, apple purée, sugar and coconut oil. Stir until melted and combined. Set aside to cool.

Sift the flour, bicarbonate of soda, cinnamon, nutmeg, cloves and sea salt into a large mixing bowl. Add the dates, figs, raisins, cranberries, orange zest, apricots and walnuts and mix well.

Add the wet mixture to the dry and stir well.

Pour into the prepared cake tin. Sprinkle the flaked almonds on the top and gently push into the batter. Bake for 1 hour or until a skewer inserted in the centre of the cake comes out clean.

Remove from the oven and allow to cool completely in the tin on a wire rack. Once cooled, remove from the tin and cut into slices.

Serve and enjoy! This cake freezes well – tightly wrap slices of cake in plastic wrap and freeze for up to 1 month.

Serves 12

125 ml (4 fl oz/½ cup) plant-based milk
320 g (11½ oz) apple purée
135 g (5 oz) rapadura sugar
60 g (2 oz) coconut oil
390 g (14 oz) gluten-free plain (all-purpose) flour
2 teaspoons bicarbonate of soda (baking soda)
1½ teaspoons ground cinnamon
½ teaspoon ground nutmeg
¼ teaspoon ground cloves
½ teaspoon ground sea salt
125 g (4½ oz) dried dates, pitted and roughly chopped
125 g (4½ oz) dried figs, roughly chopped
125 g (4½ oz) raisins
80 g (2¾ oz) dried cranberries
1 tablespoon finely grated orange zest
125 g (4½ oz) dried apricots, chopped
125 g (4½ oz) walnuts, chopped (see note)
50 g (1¾ oz) flaked almonds (see note)

NOTE
You can replace the walnuts and flaked almonds with sunflower kernels or pepitas (pumpkin seeds) for a nut-free fruitcake.

ORANGE & PASSIONFRUIT CHEESECAKE

DAIRY FREE, GLUTEN FREE, VEGAN

Put the cashew nuts for the filling in a large bowl and cover with boiling water. Soak for at least 30 minutes.

Line the base and sides of a 20 cm × 20 cm × 7 cm deep (8 in × 8 in × 3 in) springform cake tin with baking paper.

Put all the base ingredients in a food processor and blend until the mixture forms a dough and starts to stick together. Using a wet spoon, press the base mixture onto the bottom of the prepared cake tin. Freeze while you prepare the filling.

Drain and rinse the soaked cashew nuts very well. Strain the passionfruit pulp to remove seeds.

Blend the rinsed cashew nuts, passionfruit pulp and remaining filling ingredients in a food processor or high-speed blender until very smooth.

Pour the filling over the base and smooth the top. Freeze for 2 hours.

To serve, remove from the freezer and set aside at room temperature for 30 minutes. Using a warm, sharp knife, cut the cheesecake into bars. Garnish with the orange slices and drizzle over fresh passionfruit pulp.

Store the remaining cheesecake in an airtight container in the freezer for up to 1 month.

Serves 12

1 blood orange, thinly sliced, to garnish
1 fresh passionfruit, to garnish

BASE

200 g (7 oz) pepitas (pumpkin seeds)
200 g (7 oz) sunflower kernels
100 g (3½ oz) desiccated coconut
150 g (5½ oz) soft medjool dates, pitted
50 g (1¾ oz) dried apricots, roughly chopped
¼ teaspoon ground sea salt
2 teaspoons ground cinnamon
¼ teaspoon ground ginger
1 tablespoon finely grated lemon zest
30 ml (1 fl oz) freshly squeezed lemon juice

FILLING

150 g (5½ oz) raw cashew nuts
170 g (6 oz) tinned passionfruit pulp
1 tablespoon orange rind, finely grated
1 teaspoon orange extract (optional)
25 g (1 oz) goji berry powder
100 ml (3½ fl oz) freshly squeezed orange juice
130 ml (4½ fl oz) tinned coconut cream
50 ml (1¾ fl oz) rice malt syrup
80 g (2¾ oz) coconut oil

TURKISH DELIGHT CHEESECAKE

DAIRY FREE, GLUTEN FREE, VEGAN

Put the cashew nuts for the filling in a large bowl and cover with boiling water. Soak for at least 30 minutes.

Line the base and sides of a 20 cm wide × 7 cm deep (8 in × 3 in) round springform cake tin with baking paper.

For the base, blend the macadamia nuts, desiccated coconut, buckwheat kernels and cacao powder in a food processor and mix to a crumb-like texture. Add the rice malt syrup, 30 ml (1 fl oz) water and the salt and pulse until well combined. Using a wet spoon, press the mixture onto the bottom of the prepared cake tin. Freeze while you prepare the filling.

Drain and rinse the soaked cashew nuts very well. Blend the cashew nuts, rice malt syrup, lemon juice, coconut oil, coconut cream and vanilla extract in a food processor or high-speed blender until very smooth.

Divide the filling equally into two bowls. In one bowl add the cacao powder and mix until smooth. In the second bowl add the beetroot powder and rosewater extract and mix well.

Dollop small amounts of each mixture on top of the prepared base, alternating between the two colours. Tap the cake tin on the bench to smooth the top. Using a skewer, gently swirl the two fillings together to create a marble effect. Freeze for 3 hours.

Carefully remove the cheesecake from the tin, discard the baking paper and transfer to a serving plate.

For the chocolate, mix the rosewater, cacao powder, coconut oil and maple syrup until smooth. Drizzle over the edge of the cheesecake and quickly garnish the top with dried cranberries and chopped pistachios. Freeze for 15 minutes to allow the chocolate to set.

Remove from the freezer and sit at room temperature for 30 minutes before serving.

Store the remaining cheesecake in an airtight container in the freezer for up to 1 month.

Serves 12

50 g (1¾ oz) dried cranberries, to garnish
40 g (1½ oz) pistachios, chopped, to garnish

BASE
100 g (3½ oz) raw macadamia nuts
50 g (1¾ oz) unsweetened desiccated coconut
200 g (7 oz) buckwheat kernels
40 g (1½ oz/⅓ cup) cacao powder
80 ml (2½ fl oz) rice malt syrup
¼ teaspoon ground sea salt

FILLING
300 g (10½ oz) raw cashew nuts
200 ml (7 fl oz) rice malt syrup
60 ml (2 fl oz/¼ cup) freshly squeezed lemon juice
50 g (1¾ oz) coconut oil, softened
400 ml (13½ fl oz) tinned coconut cream
½ teaspoon vanilla extract
1 teaspoon cacao powder
2 teaspoons beetroot (beet) powder
2 teaspoons rosewater extract

CHOCOLATE
1 teaspoon rosewater
40 g (1½ oz/⅓ cup) cacao powder
60 g (2 oz) coconut oil, melted
20 ml (¾ fl oz) maple syrup

PEANUT BUTTER CHEESECAKE

DAIRY FREE, GLUTEN FREE, VEGAN

Jeremy, this one's for you: a rich chocolate base topped with a creamy peanut butter layer and finished with a crunchy chocolate top. A peanut butter lover's dream!

Put the cashew nuts for the filling in a large bowl and cover with boiling water. Soak for at least 30 minutes.

Line the base and sides of a 20 cm wide × 7 cm deep (8 in × 3 in) round springform cake tin with baking paper.

To make the base, blend the walnuts, buckwheat kernels, cacao powder, dates, vanilla extract and 20 ml (¾ fl oz) water in a food processor and blitz until you get the texture of crumbs that stick together when pressed. Using a wet spoon, press the mixture onto the bottom of the prepared cake tin and put in the freezer while you prepare the filling.

Drain and rinse the soaked cashew nuts very well. Blend the cashew nuts, maple syrup, pumpkin purée, peanut butter, coconut cream and vanilla extract in a food processor or high-speed blender until very smooth.

Pour the filling over the base and smooth the top evenly. Freeze for 2 hours to set.

To create the peanut topping, mix the peanuts, chocolate, maple syrup and 20 ml (¾ fl oz) water in a medium saucepan over a low heat. Mix until it's golden, fragrant and the chocolate has dissolved. Remove from the heat and add the sea salt, mixing well.

Pour the topping over the cheesecake and gently spread to create an even layer. Return the cheesecake to the freezer for 2 hours.

Carefully remove the cheesecake from the tin, discard the baking paper and transfer to a serving plate.

Allow the cheesecake to stand at room temperature for 30 minutes. Slice and enjoy!

Store the remaining cheesecake in an airtight container in the freezer for up to 1 month.

Serves 12

BASE
200 g (7 oz) raw walnuts
100 g (3½ oz) raw buckwheat kernels
40 g (1½ oz/⅓ cup) cacao powder
120 g (4½ oz) soft medjool dates, pitted
1 teaspoon vanilla extract

FILLING
300 g (10½ oz) raw cashew nuts
150 ml (5 fl oz) maple syrup
165 g (6 oz) pumpkin (squash) purée (see note)
170 g (6 oz) natural smooth peanut butter
200 ml (7 fl oz) coconut cream
1 teaspoon vanilla extract

PEANUT TOPPING
120 g (4½ oz/¾ cup) crushed peanuts
20 g (¾ oz) vegan milk chocolate, roughly chopped
30 ml (1 fl oz) maple syrup
¼ teaspoon ground sea salt

NOTE
To make the pumpkin purée, simply steam or boil the pumpkin until tender. Drain and mash to a smooth purée.

PUDDINGS
AND TARTS

PUMPKIN PECAN TART

DAIRY FREE, GLUTEN FREE, VEGAN

Pulse the sunflower kernels and almonds in a food processor until finely chopped. Add the flour, psyllium husk powder, ground cinnamon, coconut oil and coconut sugar. Process until the mixture resembles fine breadcrumbs.

Add the coconut yoghurt and vanilla extract. Process until the mixture starts to come together to form a smooth dough. Turn the mixture out onto a large piece of plastic wrap, shape into a disc and cover with plastic wrap. Refrigerate for 1 hour to rest.

To make the filling, thoroughly mix the chia seeds and 30 ml (1 fl oz) water in a small bowl. Set aside to become gelatinous.

In a clean food processor, blend the pumpkin purée, chia mixture, dates, vanilla extract, salt, cinnamon, ginger, nutmeg, coconut oil and 125 ml (4 fl oz/½ cup) water until a thick purée forms. Transfer to a large bowl and fold in three-quarters of the chopped pecans. Set aside.

Preheat the oven to 180°C (160°C fan forced/350°F).

Lightly brush a shallow 20 cm (8 in) round loose-base fluted flan (tart) tin with coconut oil. Evenly press the base into the tart tin, covering the bottom and sides.

Fill the pastry case with the filling. Smooth the surface and garnish with the remaining chopped pecans. Bake for 45 minutes or until the tart is golden and set.

Remove from the oven and set aside to cool for 30 minutes. Refrigerate for 2 hours to further set.

Best served with a dollop of coconut yoghurt.

Store in the fridge for up to 3 days.

Serves 8

coconut yoghurt, to serve
(optional)

BASE
20 g (¾ oz) raw sunflower kernels
30 g (1 oz) raw almonds
100 g (3½ oz) gluten-free plain
(all-purpose) flour
¼ teaspoon psyllium husk powder
½ teaspoon ground cinnamon
65 g (2¼ oz) coconut oil, solid
30 g (1 oz) coconut sugar
40 g (1 ½ oz) coconut yoghurt
½ teaspoon vanilla extract

FILLING
2 teaspoons chia seeds
50 g (1¾ oz) pumpkin purée
(see note)
150 g (5½ oz) soft medjool dates,
pitted
1 teaspoon vanilla extract
¼ teaspoon ground sea salt
1 teaspoon ground cinnamon
¼ teaspoon ground ginger
¼ teaspoon ground nutmeg
20 g (¾ oz) coconut oil, softened,
plus extra for greasing
165 g (6 oz/1⅓ cups) pecans,
roughly chopped

NOTE
To make the pumpkin purée,
simply steam or boil peeled
pumpkin until tender. Drain
and mash to a smooth purée.

COCONUT LIME TART

DAIRY FREE, GLUTEN FREE, VEGAN

Grease a 28.5 cm × 18 cm × 3 cm deep (11¼ in × 7 in × 1 in) loose-based rectangular flan (tart) tin with coconut oil.

Blend all the base ingredients and 30 ml (1 fl oz) water in a high-speed blender or food processor until the dough starts to stick together.

Using the back of a spoon, firmly press the base mixture evenly into the prepared tin, spreading evenly along the base and sides of the tin to form a shell. Freeze for 30 minutes.

Blend all the filling ingredients in a high-speed blender or food processor until smooth and creamy.

Pour this filling over the crust and smooth with a spatula. Freeze for 3 hours.

Once set, gently remove the tart from the tin and transfer to a serving plate. Garnish with the flaked coconut and lime zest.

Allow the tart to stand at room temperature for 15 minutes before slicing and enjoying.

Store in an airtight container in the freezer for up to 1 week.

Serves 8

coconut flakes, to garnish
lime zest, to garnish

BASE
80 g (2¾ oz) soft medjool dates, pitted
125 g (4½ oz) raw macadamia nuts
40 g (1½ oz) unsweetened desiccated coconut
75 g (2¾ oz) pepitas (pumpkin seeds)

FILLING
210 g (7½ oz) fresh avocado
90 ml (3 fl oz) freshly squeezed lime juice
1 tablespoon finely grated lime zest
160 g (5½ oz) coconut butter, softened
140 g (5 oz) tinned coconut cream
90 ml (3 fl oz) rice malt syrup

MINI CARAMEL TARTS

DAIRY FREE, GLUTEN FREE, VEGAN

Pulse the sunflower kernels and almonds in a food processor until finely chopped. Add the flour, psyllium husk powder, cinnamon, coconut oil and coconut sugar. Process until the mixture resembles fine breadcrumbs.

Add the vanilla extract and coconut yoghurt. Process until the mixture starts to come together to form a smooth dough. Turn the mixture out onto a large piece of plastic wrap, shape into a disc and cover with plastic wrap. Refrigerate for 1 hour to rest.

For the caramel, mix the coconut sugar, coconut cream, coconut oil, cornflour, milk and salt in a medium saucepan over a low heat. Whisk until the sugar has dissolved. Bring the mixture to a simmer and cook for 10–15 minutes, stirring frequently, until thickened.

Remove from the heat, then add the vanilla extract, mixing well. Set aside to cool for 15 minutes.

Preheat the oven to 180°C (160°C fan forced/350°F).

Lightly brush a twelve-hole standard muffin tin with coconut oil.

Divide the dough into twelve equal portions, then evenly press into the muffin holes, covering the base and sides.

Fill each tart base with two teaspoons of the caramel and smooth the surface. Bake for 20–30 minutes or until the tart cases are golden and set.

Remove from the oven and set aside to cool in the tin for 30 minutes. Drizzle each tart with melted chocolate and refrigerate for 2 hours.

Remove from the muffin tin and serve.

Store in an airtight container in the fridge for up to 3 days.

Makes 12 mini tarts

BASE
40 g (1½ oz) raw sunflower kernels
60 g (2 oz) raw almonds
200 g (7 oz) gluten-free plain (all-purpose) flour
½ teaspoon psyllium husk powder
1 teaspoon ground cinnamon
125 g (4½ oz) coconut oil, solid
55 g (2 oz) coconut sugar
½ teaspoon vanilla extract
85 g (3 oz) coconut yoghurt (see notes)

CARAMEL
240 g (8½ oz) coconut sugar
520 g (1 lb 2 oz) tinned coconut cream
60 g (2 oz) coconut oil
1 tablespoon cornflour (cornstarch) (see notes)
30 ml (1 fl oz) plant-based milk
1 teaspoon ground sea salt
2 teaspoons vanilla extract

TOPPING
80 g (2¾ oz) vegan milk chocolate, melted

NOTES
You can replace the coconut yoghurt with Greek yoghurt if dairy isn't your enemy.

You can replace the cornflour with arrowroot starch if you're avoiding corn.

STICKY DATE DONUTS

DAIRY FREE, GLUTEN FREE, NUT FREE, VEGAN

Preheat the oven to 190°C (170°C fan forced/375°F). Lightly grease two twelve-hole donut trays with melted coconut oil. Set aside.

In a small bowl thoroughly mix the chia seeds and 60 ml (2 fl oz/ ¼ cup) water. Set aside to become gelatinous.

Add the dates and bicarbonate of soda to a large bowl. Pour over the boiling water and stir well. Set aside for 10 minutes to soften. Use a fork to mash the dates loosely, being sure to leave some chunks of goodness.

Sift the flour, baking powder and cinnamon together. Set aside.

Beat the coconut cream, vanilla extract and sugar together with an electric mixer until creamy. Add the chia mixture and beat until combined.

Fold in the date mixture with a spatula. Gently fold in the flour mixture.

Evenly fill eighteen donut moulds to two-thirds full. Bake for 30 minutes or until a skewer inserted into a donut comes out clean.

To make the sauce, put the coconut oil, coconut sugar, coconut cream, cornflour and sea salt in a small saucepan over a low heat, stirring frequently to dissolve the sugar. Bring the mixture to a simmer and cook for 5 minutes, stirring frequently, until thickened slightly. Remove from the heat and add the vanilla extract, mixing well. Set aside to cool for 10 minutes.

To serve, remove the donuts from the trays. Drizzle the sauce over the top and add a sprinkle of dried dates.

Serve and enjoy.

Makes 18 donuts

DONUTS

25 g (1 oz) chia seeds
180 g (6½ oz) dried dates, pitted
  and roughly chopped
½ teaspoon bicarbonate of soda
  (baking soda)
300 ml (10 fl oz) boiling water
150 g (5½ oz) gluten-free plain
  (all-purpose) flour
1¼ teaspoon baking powder
1 teaspoon ground cinnamon
60 g (2 oz) tinned coconut cream
1 teaspoon vanilla extract
175 g (6 oz) coconut sugar

SAUCE

30 g (1 oz) coconut oil
120 g (4½ oz) coconut sugar
260 g (9 oz) tinned coconut cream
2 teaspoons cornflour (cornstarch)
  (see note)
½ teaspoon ground sea salt
1 teaspoon vanilla extract

TOPPING

60 g (2 oz) dried dates, pitted and
  roughly chopped

NOTE

You can replace the cornflour with arrowroot starch.

JAFFA PUDDING

DAIRY FREE, GLUTEN FREE, NUT FREE, VEGAN

I used to love Jaffas, so I've reinvented the classic treat in this gooey pudding. Best served fresh and hot.

Preheat the oven to 190°C (170°C fan forced/375°F). Lightly grease a 20.8 cm × 8.6 cm deep (8 in × 3¼ in) ring (bundt) tin with coconut oil. Set aside.

In a small bowl thoroughly mix the chia seeds and 60 ml (2 fl oz/ ¼ cup) water. Set aside to become gelatinous.

Put the dates and bicarbonate of soda in a large bowl. Pour over the boiling water and orange juice and stir well. Set aside for 10 minutes to soften. Transfer to a high-speed blender and mix until it becomes a smooth purée.

Sift the flour, baking powder and cacao powder together. Set aside.

Beat the coconut cream, vanilla extract and sugar together with an electric mixer until creamy. Add the chia mixture and orange zest and beat until combined. Add the date purée and beat well. Gently fold in the flour mixture with a spatula.

Pour into the prepared tin. Bake for 60–75 minutes or until a skewer inserted into the centre of the pudding comes out with a few moist crumbs attached.

Cool in the tin for 5 minutes before removing and transferring to a serving plate.

To make the sauce, stir the coconut oil, rice malt syrup, coconut cream, orange juice, orange zest and cornflour in a small saucepan over a low heat. Stir well and bring the mixture to a simmer. Cook for 5 minutes, stirring frequently until thickened.

Remove from the heat. Add the vanilla extract and goji powder and mix well. Set aside to cool for 10 minutes.

Pour the sauce over the warm pudding and garnish with the fine orange peel curls.

Store the remaining pudding in an airtight container in the fridge for up to 3 days.

Serves 6

fine orange peel curls, to garnish

PUDDING

25 g (1 oz) chia seeds
180 g (6½ oz) dried dates, pitted and roughly chopped
½ teaspoon bicarbonate of soda (baking soda)
250 ml (8½ fl oz/1 cup) boiling water
100 ml (3½ fl oz) orange juice
150 g (5½ oz) gluten-free plain (all-purpose) flour
1¼ teaspoon baking powder
30 g (1 oz/¼ cup) cacao powder
60 g (2 oz) tinned coconut cream
1 teaspoon vanilla extract
175 g (6 oz) coconut sugar
1 tablespoon finely grated orange zest

SAUCE

3 teaspoons coconut oil, plus extra for greasing
25 ml (¾ fl oz) rice malt syrup
75 g (2¾ oz) tinned coconut cream
40 ml (1¼ fl oz) freshly squeezed orange juice
1 tablespoon finely grated orange zest
1 teaspoon cornflour (cornstarch) (see note)
½ teaspoon vanilla extract
1 teaspoon goji berry powder

NOTE
You can replace the cornflour with arrowroot starch.

APPLE & APRICOT CRUMBLE

DAIRY FREE, GLUTEN FREE, VEGAN

Preheat the oven to 180°C (160°C fan forced/350°F).

Cut the apple into 2 cm (¾ in) dice and combine with the remaining filling ingredients in a large bowl. Transfer to a 1.5 litre (51fl oz/6 cup) capacity ovenproof dish.

For the crumble, pulse the walnuts in a food processor until they form a flour. Add the remaining ingredients and pulse until a dough forms.

Tip the mixture out onto a floured bench and bring together with your hands to form a flat disc. Wrap in plastic wrap and freeze for 30 minutes.

Once chilled, crumble the dough evenly over the apple mixture. Top with chopped pistachios.

Bake for 40–50 minutes or until golden and the apple is cooked. Serve hot or warm. Delicious with Chai ice cream (page 100).

Serves 6

FILLING
400 g (14 oz) raw green apples (see note)
40 ml (1¼ fl oz) freshly squeezed orange juice
100 g (3½ oz) sultanas (golden raisins)
160 g (5½ oz) dried apricots, roughly chopped
60 g (2 oz) rapadura sugar
1 teaspoon vanilla extract
1 teaspoon ground cinnamon
½ teaspoon arrowroot starch

CRUMBLE
75 g (2¾ oz) raw walnuts
200 g (7 oz) gluten-free plain (all-purpose) flour
¾ teaspoon psyllium husk
55 g (2 oz) rapadura sugar
80 g (2¾ oz) coconut oil
125 g (4½ oz/½ cup) tinned coconut cream
1 teaspoon apple cider vinegar
¼ teaspoon ground nutmeg
¼ teaspoon ground ginger

TOPPING
30 g (1 oz) raw pistachio nuts, chopped

NOTE
Feel free to use any fruit you like! Pears or peaches would also work well.

OTHER
TREATS

DONUTS

DAIRY FREE, GLUTEN FREE, VEGAN

Preheat the oven to 180°C (160°C fan forced/350°F).

Grease a twelve-hole donut tin with coconut oil. Set aside.

Drain the chickpeas, reserving 120 ml (4½ fl oz) of the liquid (aquafaba). Transfer the chickpeas to a sealed container and refrigerate for another use. Whisk the chickpea aquafaba until frothy.

In a large bowl, whisk the dry donut ingredients to combine. Make a well in the centre and add the frothy aquafaba, apple cider vinegar, vanilla extract and milk. Mix until just combined.

Spoon the batter evenly into the prepared donut tin, filling the moulds three-quarters of the way up. Bake for 10 minutes or until lightly golden and puffed. Cool in the tin for 5 minutes, then transfer to a cooling rack.

Dip some donuts into the melted chocolate and return to the cooling rack to set. Dip other donuts into the melted coconut butter and return to the cooling rack to set. Drizzle donuts with peanut butter, freeze-dried strawberries, coconut flakes and crushed peanuts. Get creative and decorate!

Serve and enjoy! Donuts are best eaten fresh.

Makes 12 small donuts

DONUTS

400 g (14 oz) tin salt-free chickpeas

165 g (6 oz) gluten-free plain (all-purpose) flour

65 g (2¼ oz) rapadura sugar

¼ teaspoon ground nutmeg

1 teaspoon baking powder

1 teaspoon bicarbonate of soda (baking soda)

1 teaspoon apple cider vinegar

1 teaspoon vanilla extract

125 ml (4 fl oz/½ cup) plant-based milk

TOPPINGS

100 g (3½ oz) vegan milk chocolate, melted

150 g (5½ oz) coconut butter, melted

35 g (1¼ oz) smooth peanut butter

30 g (1 oz) freeze-dried strawberries, crushed

30 g (1 oz) coconut flakes

30 g (1 oz) crushed peanuts

NUTTER BUTTER CUPS

DAIRY FREE, GLUTEN FREE, VEGAN

Line a twelve-hole standard muffin tin with nine silicone liners.

Mix half the cacao powder, half the maple syrup and half the melted coconut oil together until smooth.

With a small spoon, evenly distribute the chocolate mixture into the silicone liners. Lightly drop the muffin tin on the bench a few times to flatten the chocolate. Freeze for 15 minutes.

To make the peanut layer, add all the ingredients to a small saucepan. Mix over a low heat until the sugar has dissolved. Drop a spoonful of the peanut mixture over the chilled chocolate layer in each of the silicone liners, and spread to create an even layer. Freeze for 15 minutes.

Mix the remaining cacao powder, maple syrup and coconut oil together. Spoon over the peanut layer and tap the tray on the bench again to flatten the last layer. Freeze for a further 15 minutes.

Remove each cup from its silicone liner and serve.

The cups will keep in the freezer for up to 1 month.

Makes 9

CHOCOLATE
100 g (3½ oz) cacao powder
100 ml (3½ fl oz) maple syrup
120 g (4½ oz) coconut oil, melted

PEANUT LAYER (SEE NOTE)
140 g (5 oz) smooth peanut butter
50 g (1¾ oz) coconut sugar
100 g (3½ oz) coconut
    condensed milk

NOTE
Feel free to use any filling you like! Try a seed butter if you are avoiding nuts.

PANCAKES

DAIRY FREE, GLUTEN FREE, NUT FREE, VEGAN

Combine all the ingredients in a blender until smooth. Set batter aside for 10 minutes to thicken.

Heat a non-stick pan over a medium heat and lightly coat with coconut oil.

Drop spoonfuls of batter onto the pan and wait until bubbles form before flipping each pancake. Cook until golden on both sides.

Serve with Chocolate hazelnut butter (below), pure maple syrup or your choice of toppings.

FLAVOUR COMBINATIONS

Blueberry: Stir 155 g (5½ oz/1 cup) blueberries into the pancake batter for a burst of sweetness.

Carrot cake: Stir 1 teaspoon of cinnamon and 1 tablespoon of sultanas into the batter with 40 g (1½ oz/¼ cup) grated carrot before cooking.

Red velvet: Stir 1 teaspoon of beetroot (beet) powder into the batter and top the finished pancakes with coconut yoghurt and shredded coconut.

Makes 10 small pancakes

90 g (3 oz) quinoa flakes
150 g (5½ oz) gluten-free plain (all-purpose) flour
1 teaspoon psyllium husk
1 tablespoon baking powder
2 teaspoons vanilla extract
350 ml (6 fl oz) plant-based milk
2 medjool dates (approx. 40 g/ 1½ oz), pitted
150 g (5½ oz) apple purée (see note)
coconut oil, for frying
pure maple syrup, to serve (optional)

NOTE
You can substitute solidified coconut cream for the apple purée if needed.

CHOCOLATE HAZELNUT BUTTER

DAIRY FREE, GLUTEN FREE, VEGAN

In a food processor or high-powered blender, blend the hazelnuts until they have a creamy butter consistency. Occasionally scrape down the sides of the bowl. Have patience — it will eventually turn to butter. Add the remaining ingredients and blend until silky smooth.

Serve on top of pancakes, a dollop in smoothies, smeared on toast — the sky is the limit!

Store in the fridge for up to 1 month.

250 g (9 oz) dry-roasted hazelnuts
25 g (1 oz) cacao powder
25 ml (¾ fl oz) vanilla extract
¼ teaspoon ground sea salt
120 ml (4 fl oz) plant-based milk
130 g (4½ oz) soft medjool dates, pitted

ICE CREAM

DAIRY FREE, GLUTEN FREE, NUT FREE, VEGAN

Line a loaf (bar) tin or 1-litre (34 fl oz/4 cup) ice cream tub with baking paper.

Using an electric mixer, whisk together all the ingredients for 15 minutes or until soft peaks form. You want the consistency of whipped cream.

Add desired flavours (see below) and whisk to combine.

Transfer the mixture to the prepared container. Cover with a lid or plastic wrap and foil. Freeze overnight.

Remove the ice cream from the freezer 20 minutes prior to scooping. Enjoy!

Makes approximately 1 litre (34 fl oz/4 cups)

200 g (7 oz) coconut condensed milk
600 ml (20½ fl oz) tinned coconut cream
1 teaspoon vanilla extract

NOTES
Get creative with flavours and try your own combinations.

This ice cream is best served soon after initial freezing time, as it tends to go solid after a few days.

ICE-CREAM FLAVOURS

CHAI
1 teaspoon cinnamon
¼ teaspoon ginger
¼ teaspoon nutmeg

PEPPERMINT
½ teaspoon peppermint extract
¼ teaspoon spirulina
¼ teaspoon vegan green food colouring
½ teaspoon cacao powder

ESPRESSO
2 teaspoons ground espresso
20 g (¾ oz) cacao powder

STRAWBERRY
100 g (3½ oz) puréed strawberries
50 g (1¾ oz) vegan white chocolate chips

RUM & RAISIN
150 g (5½ oz) raisins
50 ml (1¾ fl oz) dark sweet rum

Bring the raisins and rum to a boil in a saucepan over a medium heat. Remove from the heat and allow to cool. Fold through the ice cream base mixture.

SALTED CARAMEL
130 g (4½ oz) soft medjool dates, pitted
½ teaspoon ground sea salt

Blend the dates in a food processor with the salt until a purée forms, adding water if needed. Stir the purée through the ice cream base mixture.

CHURROS

DAIRY FREE, GLUTEN FREE, NUT FREE, VEGAN

For the dipping sauce, mix the coconut sugar, coconut cream and sea salt in a small saucepan over a low heat, frequently stirring to dissolve the sugar. Bring the mixture to a simmer and cook for 5 minutes. Remove from the heat and add the vanilla extract, mixing well. Set aside to cool.

For the churros, preheat the oven to 200°C (180°C fan forced/400°F). Line a large 38 cm × 25 cm (15 in × 10 in) baking tray (cookie sheet) with baking paper.

In a medium saucepan over a low heat stir 250 ml (8½ fl oz/1 cup) water, 30 g (1¼ oz) of the sugar and the salt until they have dissolved. Remove from the heat and add the coconut oil and vanilla extract, mixing well. Add the flour and psyllium husk and stir until combined.

Transfer the mixture to a piping (icing) bag with a large star tip. Pipe long strips of dough onto the prepared baking tray, leaving a 3 cm (1 in) space between each churro. You can pipe the churros to be as long as you like — get creative!

Bake for 15–20 minutes or until the churros are nicely puffed and golden.

Combine the remaining sugar and ground cinnamon in a sealable bag and shake to combine. One by one, put the churros inside the bag and shake to evenly coat. Serve immediately alongside the caramel dipping sauce and melted chocolate.

Makes 12 large churros

70 g (2½ oz) coconut milk
   chocolate, melted, to serve

CARAMEL DIPPING SAUCE (SEE NOTE)
30 g (1 oz) coconut sugar
65 g (2¼ oz) tinned coconut cream
¼ teaspoon ground sea salt
¼ teaspoon vanilla extract

CHURROS
60 g (2 oz) rapadura sugar
½ teaspoon ground sea salt
30 g (1 oz) coconut oil
1 teaspoon vanilla extract
215 g (7½ oz) gluten-free plain
   (all-purpose) flour
1 teaspoon psyllium husk
1 teaspoon ground cinnamon

NOTE
Feel free to use any dipping sauce you like!

CHOCOLATE CHIP COOKIES

DAIRY FREE, GLUTEN FREE, NUT FREE, VEGAN

In a small bowl, thoroughly mix the chia seeds and 20 ml (¾ fl oz) water. Set aside to become gelatinous.

In a bowl, beat the coconut oil and sugar with an electric mixer for 3–4 minutes until creamy and combined. Add the chia mixture and vanilla extract, and beat until well combined.

In a large bowl, sift the flour, baking powder and bicarbonate of soda. Mix in the wet ingredients using a spatula until combined. Gently fold through the chocolate chunks and sea salt. Refrigerate the dough for 20 minutes.

Preheat the oven to 180°C (160°C fan forced/350°F). Line two 38 cm × 25 cm (15 in × 10 in) baking trays (cookie sheets) with baking paper.

Using wet hands, scoop a tablespoon of the mixture, roll it into a ball and place on the baking tray. Repeat with the remaining mixture. Be sure to leave plenty of room between each cookie, as the dough will spread.

Bake for 10–12 minutes.

Remove from the oven and cool on a wire rack before eating.

Store the cookies in the fridge for up to 4 days.

Makes 16

1 teaspoon chia seeds
80 g (2¾ oz) coconut oil
155 g (5½ oz) rapadura sugar
1 teaspoon vanilla extract
150 g (5½ oz) gluten-free plain (all-purpose) flour
½ teaspoon baking powder
¼ teaspoon bicarbonate of soda (baking soda)
60 g (2 oz) vegan chocolate, cut into 2 cm (¾ in) chunks
¼ teaspoon ground sea salt

SALTED CARAMEL COOKIES FOR TWO

DAIRY FREE, GLUTEN FREE, NUT FREE, VEGAN

Soft-centred jumbo cookies for those lazy nights when you need a quick and easy treat. Perfectly paired with a cup of tea, one for me and one for you.

Preheat the oven to 180°C (160°C fan forced/350°F). Line a 38 cm × 25 cm (15 in × 10 in) baking tray (cookie sheet) with baking paper.

In a small bowl, thoroughly mix the chia seeds with 30 ml (1 fl oz) water. Set aside to become gelatinous.

Add all the remaining ingredients except the chocolate to a large bowl. Mix in the chia mixture until a wet dough forms. Fold in half of the chopped chocolate.

Split the dough into two and shape into two large discs on the baking tray. Stud the dough with remaining chocolate.

Bake for 20 minutes for a soft, gooey cookie.

Makes 2 jumbo cookies

1 tablespoon chia seeds
60 g (2 oz) tinned coconut cream
60 g (2 oz) coconut sugar
¼ teaspoon ground sea salt
½ teaspoon vanilla extract
100 g (3½ oz) brown rice flour
¼ teaspoon bicarbonate of soda (baking soda)
50 g (1¾ oz) dairy-free salted caramel chocolate, roughly chopped

Not a fan of salted caramel? No problem! Here are some other flavour combinations:

STICKY DATE
Replace the chocolate with 50 g (1¾ oz/¼ cup) chopped dates, 30 g (1 oz/¼ cup) chopped pecans and 1 teaspoon of cinnamon.

WHITE CHOCOLATE
Replace the caramel chocolate with 25 g (1 oz/¼ cup) vegan white choc chips, 25 g (1 oz/¼ cup) dried cranberries and 25 g (1 oz/¼ cup) chopped macadamia nuts.

CHOC CHIP
Replace the caramel chocolate with vegan milk chocolate.

RAINBOW MERINGUE

DAIRY FREE, GLUTEN FREE, NUT FREE, VEGAN

Meringue with no eggs? The transformation of chickpea water (aquafaba) to fluffy meringue is genius. I've discovered caster sugar works best for this recipe — one of the only times I use refined sugar.

Preheat the oven to 100°C (80°C fan forced/200°F). Prepare a large clean glass or metal mixing bowl that's completely clean and free of grease.

Drain the chickpeas, reserving 145 ml (5 fl oz) of the liquid (aquafaba). Transfer the chickpeas to a sealed container and refrigerate for another use. Using an electric mixer, whisk the chickpea aquafaba and cream of tartar on medium speed until stiff peaks form. Continue mixing, adding the sugar one tablespoon at a time until it's all incorporated. Whisk for a further minute, add the vanilla extract and whisk briefly again.

Working quickly, divide the mixture into three clean bowls. To make the yellow meringue, add a drop of yellow food colouring to one of the bowls and gently fold it through the meringue. Repeat with the remaining bowls of meringue and the pink and blue food colourings.

Prepare a piping (icing) bag with a large star-shaped nozzle. Spoon a dollop of yellow meringue into the piping (icing) bag, top with pink meringue and then blue. Repeat until all the meringue is used. Be gentle with the mixture so it doesn't deflate.

Line a large baking tray (cookie sheet) with baking paper. Pipe small circles onto the baking paper. Be sure to only create one even layer so it bakes evenly.

Bake for 3½ hours or until the meringues feel firm on the outside. Do not open the door to tap the meringues until at least 2 hours have passed.

Leave the cooked meringues in the oven to cool for 1½–2 hours, which will allow the meringues to firm up inside. Do not open the oven door.

Once cool, remove the meringues from the oven and slide onto a serving platter. Serve with the yoghurt, mixed berries and nuts.

Store the meringues in an airtight container in the fridge for 4–5 days. If they start to go sticky before this, dry them out in an oven preheated to 100°C (80°C fan forced/200°F) for 20–30 minutes.

Serves 12

MERINGUE
400 g (14 oz) tin salt-free chickpeas, chilled
½ teaspoon cream of tartar
145 g (5 oz) caster (superfine) sugar (see note)
½ teaspoon vanilla extract
vegan yellow food colouring
vegan pink food colouring
vegan blue food colouring

OPTIONAL GARNISHES
coconut yoghurt, to serve
fresh mixed berries, to serve
chopped hazelnuts

NOTE
You can substitute 145 g (5 oz) rapadura sugar mixed with 1 teaspoon arrowroot starch for the caster sugar. It will still work, but it will produce a flatter meringue with a less airy texture.

BREAKFAST SMOOTHIE

DAIRY FREE, GLUTEN FREE, VEGAN

Blend all the smoothie ingredients in a high-speed blender until thick and smooth.

Pour into two glasses and enjoy.

Serves 2

40 g (1½ oz) gluten-free rolled oats (see notes)
400 ml (13½ fl oz) plant-based milk (see notes)
100 g (3½ oz) frozen pear, cored
30 g (1 oz) almond butter
¼ teaspoon vanilla extract

NOTES
You can use any plant-based milk in this recipe. I love using coconut milk.

You can also use your favourite gluten-free granola or muesli instead of oats.

CHERRY CHOCOLATE SMOOTHIE

DAIRY FREE, GLUTEN FREE, NUT FREE, VEGAN

This tastes like a chocolate thickshake. You know, the one drink you feel naughty ordering from your local cafe. Now you can drink up and not feel one ounce of guilt. Thank me later.

Blend all the ingredients in a high-speed blender until thick and smooth.

Pour into two glasses and enjoy.

Serves 2

350 g (12½ oz) frozen cherries
40 g (1½ oz) fresh spinach leaves
65 g (2¼ oz) medjool dates, pitted
25 g (1 oz) cacao powder
¼ teaspoon vanilla extract
400 ml (13½ fl oz) coconut milk (see note)
20 g (¾ oz) chia seeds

NOTE
I love using coconut milk, but you can use any plant-based milk in this recipe.

STRAWBERRIES & CREAM SMOOTHIE

DAIRY FREE, GLUTEN FREE, NUT FREE, VEGAN

Blend the oats, frozen strawberries, dates, vanilla extract and coconut milk in a high-speed blender until thick and smooth.

Place a small amount of the smoothie in the bottom of two mason jars. Top with some of the coconut yoghurt and more smoothie. Continue this process until you have used all the smoothie and coconut yoghurt. Top with strawberries and flaked coconut. Serve with a spoon.

Serves 2

50 g (1¾ oz) gluten-free oats

320 g (11½ oz) frozen strawberries

30 g (1 oz) soft medjool dates, pitted

¼ teaspoon vanilla extract

300 ml (10 fl oz) coconut milk (see note)

200 g (7 oz) coconut yoghurt

fresh strawberries, to serve

flaked coconut, to serve

NOTE
I love using coconut milk, but you can use any plant-based milk in this recipe.

SWEET SUBSTITUTES

Let's talk about pantry essentials: sugar, flour, eggs, oil, dairy and nuts.
The following pages will discuss some must-have ingredients; these
are the favourite substitutes that I use in almost all my cakes and desserts.

With this simple guide, you can adapt any recipe to suit your own tastes or
allergies, and make adjustments that suit your lifestyle. Every person is different,
so it's important to read ingredient labels and any dietary advice carefully.

Okay, let's begin! Tie on a fresh apron and dive into the kitchen with a healthy
curiosity. Get ready to try something tasty and brand new!

Sugar.

A spoonful might help the medicine go down, but with rising amounts hidden in our meals, refined sugar has become sickly sweet.

Sweetness doesn't have to be the enemy. If you explore beyond the processed sources, you'll uncover natural and wholesome sweeteners. The following examples are my favourite sugar alternatives, which can be picked up at your local supermarket or health food store.

Fall in love with natural sugars and find creative uses beyond the recipes in this book. Make your life sweet, golden and nutritious.

Alternative Sweeteners

Blackstrap Molasses

Best for: gingerbread, muesli cookies, oatmeal bars

How to: For 220 g (8 oz/1 cup) of white sugar, use 330 ml (11 fl oz/1⅓ cups) of blackstrap molasses. Replace no more than half the sugar in a recipe with blackstrap molasses and be careful of your flavours. You will also need to add ½ teaspoon of bicarbonate of soda (baking soda) for each cup of molasses used.

Tips: Containing all the nutrients stripped from the sugar cane, blackstrap molasses is full of copper, iron, calcium, vitamin B6 and potassium. This dark, velvety liquid is fantastic for vegans and vegetarians.

Although it has an incredible nutritional profile, this thick syrup has an adamant flavour that can be hard on the tastebuds and also proves difficult when substituting in desserts. Blackstrap molasses works best when used in earthy recipes such as those listed above.

Brown Rice Syrup (Rice Malt Syrup)

Best for: brownies, candies, raw treats

How to: Replace 220 g (8 oz/1 cup) of white sugar with 310 ml (10½ fl oz/ 1¼ cups) of brown rice syrup. You will also need to reduce the liquid in the recipe by around 3 tablespoons and add $^1/_{16}$ teaspoon of bicarbonate of soda (baking soda). Brown rice syrup can be swapped 1:1 cup for liquid sugars in recipes.

Tips: Golden and thick, this toffee-flavoured syrup is created by culturing brown rice and then reducing it down to a syrup. It has similar properties to golden syrup and works well as a binder in raw treats.

Brown rice syrup isn't as sweet as white sugar and refuses to 'cream' in recipes. It also comes with a pretty steep price tag. Use it in recipes when you have no maple syrup on hand and you want less sweetness in your dessert.

Coconut Nectar

Best for: raw desserts, cakes, baked treats

How to: Coconut nectar has a very thick, syrupy texture and is best swapped 1:1 cup in recipes that ask for maple syrup, corn syrup or brown rice syrup. However, you can also use 125 ml (4 fl oz/½ cup) of coconut nectar to replace 220 g (8 oz/1 cup) of granulated sugar, but it will take some experimenting.

Tips: Coconut nectar comes from coconut palm blossoms and is a fabulous low-GI sugar alternative. This mineral-rich nectar provides a broad spectrum of amino acids and can help you feel fuller for longer. I find coconut nectar sweeter than brown rice syrup with a more toffee/caramel-like flavour.

Just like other liquid sugars, coconut nectar won't cream in recipes and can be quite expensive. However, the sticky consistency of this syrup makes it a fantastic binding ingredient for raw desserts, cakes and baked treats.

Coconut Sugar

Best for: cookies, shortbreads, bread, cakes

How to: Swap 1:1 cup for white sugar or soft brown sugar.

To make caster (superfine) sugar: Pulse coconut sugar a few times in a food processor until you see a fine texture.

To make icing (powdered) sugar: Put 140 g (5 oz/1 cup) of coconut sugar and 1 tablespoon of arrowroot starch, cornflour (cornstarch), tapioca flour or potato starch in a high-speed blender. Start with a low speed and work your way up to the highest speed. Blend until you see a powdered sugar. Transfer to a sealed glass jar and store in your pantry until needed.

Tips: Compensate for the dry texture of coconut sugar with an additional tablespoon or two of moist ingredients. Mashed sweet potato and apple sauce are perfect for this. Also, keep an eye on your baked goods: they can cook faster with coconut sugar.

Dried Fruit

Best for: cookies, bars, raw treats, brownies

How to: Chopped dried fruits can replace ¼ of the granulated sugar in a recipe. Unfortunately, unless it's a raw treat, you can't adequately replace all granulated sugar in a baking recipe with dried fruit. Puréed dried fruits can be swapped 1:1 cup with liquid sugar.

Tips: Sweet dried fruit such as dates, figs, apricots and prunes can add significant sweetness to a recipe. Dried fruit will also add fibre, binding and moisture to the recipe. Chop the dried fruit into small pieces for bursts of sweetness in your baked goods, or soak overnight in water and then purée for a liquid sugar substitute.

Maple Syrup

Best for: candy, puddings, ice cream, muesli, raw treats

How to: In baking, for every 220 g (8 oz/1 cup) of granulated sugar, substitute 190 ml (6½ fl oz/¾ cup) of maple syrup. You will also need to lower the baking temperature of your oven by 4°C (25°F), add ¼ teaspoon of bicarbonate of soda (baking soda) and reduce the liquids in your recipe by 3 tablespoons. Maple syrup can be swapped 1:1 cup for other liquid sweeteners in recipes.

Tips: Buy pure, high-quality maple syrup and not the processed, high fructose corn syrup version. Pure maple syrup will cost a little more, but there's beneficial calcium, potassium, sodium and copper in each drop. Look for grade B maple syrup for a deeper and richer flavour.

Unfortunately, like all liquid sugars, maple syrup doesn't cream in a recipe the way granulated sugar does, and can cause your baked goods to brown faster. High-quality maple syrup can also be quite expensive.

Medjool Dates

Best for: brownies, pie crusts, cookies, raw treats, muesli bars

How to: Add 180 g (6½ oz/1 cup) of pitted medjool dates and 60 ml (2 fl oz/ ¼ cup) of water to a food processor or blender and mix to a thick purée. Substitute 120 g (4½ oz/⅔ cup) of date purée for 220 g (8 oz/1 cup) of regular white sugar. Make sure you remove the pits from your fresh dates before puréeing!

Tips: A bunch of medjool dates can provide a natural caramel flavour and subtle vanilla sweetness to your dessert. Full of iron, potassium, calcium, minerals and fibre, with a low GI index, medjool dates are an excellent binding agent. They can be found in the fresh produce section of your supermarket. Medjool dates are soft, gooey and sticky compared to dried dates.

Dates produce a subtle, complex flavour in baked goods. Pair them with a complementary recipe such as fruit bread, caramel treats, oatmeal bars, chocolate sweets or carrot cakes for a delicious dessert.

Puréed Fruits or Vegetables

Best for: bread, loaves, muffins, cakes

How to: Use 120 g (4½/½ cup) fruit or vegetable purée to replace 220 g (8 oz/1 cup) of sugar. Decrease the other liquid ingredients by 3 tablespoons.

Tips: One of my favourite ways to sweeten desserts is with fruit or vegetables. A spoonful of apple sauce, mashed banana, mashed sweet potato and puréed berries are just some of the alternatives that can add natural sweetness and moisture to your baking.

Fruit can add a distinctive flavour to baked goods, so it's important to pair the ingredients well for the ultimate taste sensation. Matching mashed pineapple with carrot cake or sweet potato with chocolate cake are two great examples. I find apple sauce and sweet potato provide a sugar hit without the fruity taste.

Puréed fruit or vegetables will alter the texture of your baked goods and provide an extra wet batter and moist final dessert. It takes some experimenting to get your ratios right, and you may find that your baked goods will cook faster and won't rise as high.

Rapadura Sugar

Best for: cookies, shortbreads, bread, pastries, cakes

How to: Swap 1:1 cup rapadura sugar for white sugar.

Tips: Minimally processed, high in vitamins and minerals and a fantastic substitute for white sugar, rapadura sugar has a rich, deep toffee flavour and larger crystals than regular sugar. It will also give your baked goods a rich golden colour. To retain a soft baked good, dissolve the sugar in the recipe's liquid component for approximately five minutes before adding to the remaining ingredients. Unlike coconut sugar, rapadura won't alter the texture of your dessert.

To make caster (superfine) sugar: Pulse rapadura sugar a few times in a food processor until you see a fine texture.

To make icing (powdered) sugar: Put 160 g (5½ oz/1 cup) of rapadura sugar and 1 tablespoon of arrowroot starch, cornflour (cornstarch), tapioca flour or potato starch in a high-speed blender. Start with a low speed and work your way up to the highest speed. Blend until you see a powdered sugar. Transfer to a sealed glass jar and store in your pantry until you need it.

Stevia

Best for: any recipe!

How to: Substitute 220 g (8 oz/1 cup) of sugar with 1 teaspoon of green leaf stevia powder. For every cup of sugar substituted with stevia, add 80 g (2¾ oz/⅓ cup) of a bulking agent, such as fruit purée, apple sauce or yoghurt, to the recipe.

Tips: It's important when buying stevia that you choose green leaf stevia powder and not the white bleached powder you see in supermarkets. Supermarket stevia is often mixed with other artificial sweeteners, whereas green leaf stevia consists of the whole leaf dried at low temperatures, then ground into a fine powder. It's an all-natural sweetener that is thirty times sweeter than sugar.

As stevia is so potent, it can be hard to get the balance right when using it in recipes. The green leaf powder can also be more expensive; however, you use so little per recipe that it becomes an economical choice. It may also colour your dessert green!

Sugar Conversions

White Sugar Conversion

SWEETENER	TO REPLACE 220 g (8 oz/ 1 cup) OF WHITE SUGAR	LIQUID IN RECIPE	TIPS
Blackstrap molasses	330 ml (11 fl oz/ 1⅓ cups) + ½ teaspoon of bicarbonate of soda (baking soda)		Replace no more than half the sugar with molasses
Brown rice syrup	310 ml (10½ fl oz/ 1¼ cups) + $1/16$ teaspoon of bicarbonate of soda (baking soda)	Reduce by 3 tablespoons	
Coconut nectar	125 ml (4 fl oz/½ cup)		
Coconut sugar	140 g (5 oz/1 cup)		
Dried fruit	35 g (1¼ oz/¼ cup) approximately		Replace no more than a quarter of the sugar with dried fruit
Maple syrup	190 ml (6½ fl oz/ ¾ cup) + ¼ teaspoon of bicarbonate of soda (baking soda)	Reduce by 3 tablespoons	Lower the oven temperature by 4°C (25° F)
Medjool dates	120 g (4½ oz/⅔ cup) date purée		Purée 180 g (6½ oz 1 cup) medjool dates and 60 ml (2 fl oz/ ¼ cup) water
Pureed fruit or vegetables	120 g (4½ g/½ cup)	Reduce by 3 tablespoons	
Rapadura sugar	160 g (5½ oz/1 cup)		
Stevia	1 teaspoon + 80 g (2¾ oz/ ⅓ cup) bulking agent		Calculating quantities can be tricky, so you'll need to experiment.

Brown Sugar Conversion

SWEETENER	TO REPLACE 200 g (7 oz/1 cup) BROWN SUGAR
Coconut sugar	140 g (5 oz/1 cup)
Rapadura sugar	160 g (5½ oz/1 cup)

Icing (Powdered) Sugar Conversion

SWEETENER	TO REPLACE 125 g (4½ oz/1 cup) ICING (POWDERED) SUGAR	TIPS
Coconut sugar	140 g (5 oz/1 cup) coconut sugar + 1 tablespoon starch	I like to use arrowroot or cornflour as my starch
Rapadura sugar	160 g (5½ oz/1 cup) rapadura sugar + 1 tablespoon starch	Blend in a high-speed blender or food processor until a powder forms

Liquid Sugar Conversion

SWEETENER	SWAP 1:1 CUP
Maple syrup	Brown rice syrup Coconut nectar Pureed dried fruit
Honey	Brown rice syrup Maple syrup Coconut nectar Pureed dried fruit
Corn syrup	Brown rice syrup Maple syrup Coconut nectar
Golden syrup	Brown rice syrup Maple syrup Coconut nectar Molasses

Flour.

Wheat flour can be a sensitive topic. Beyond the stress it causes coeliacs, wheat substitutes can make gluten-free baking a gamble.

When cooking with alternative flours, it's important to mix and match the weights of the flours as best as possible. This helps avoid the dreaded 'gummy texture'. I'll discuss each weight type in detail, so you can perfect your signature gluten-free blend.

Lightweight Flours (Starch)

Lightweight flours are also known as starches. These are ideal for binding ingredients and adding lightness to the final result. These starches cannot be used alone in baking and are best combined with mediumweight and heavyweight flours. Here are my favourites.

Arrowroot starch or tapioca flour: This easy-to-digest starch is light and fantastic for thickening and binding ingredients together. It will also add lightness and crispness to cookies.

Cornflour (cornstarch): Great for thickening sauces and adding a fluffy texture to recipes. When shopping for cornflour be on the lookout for non-GMO brands and check carefully to make sure it's gluten free. It's best used when combined with another starch and one or two mediumweight flours and an optional heavyweight flour.

Potato starch: Not to be confused with potato flour, potato starch adds lightness, moisture and lift to recipes. It's also fantastic at providing thickness and stability to vegan icing. To avoid the potato flavour, it's best used when combined with another starch plus one or two mediumweight flours and an optional heavyweight flour.

Sweet rice flour: Not to be confused with white rice flour, sweet rice flour is made from short-grain glutinous rice rather than medium-grain rice. Like other starches, it's extremely efficient for thickening sauces or binding ingredients. When baking, it's best used when combined with mediumweight and heavyweight flours.

Mediumweight Flours

Mediumweight flours help to lighten the heavyweight flours and soften the crumb in your recipes. They can be used alone or paired with one or two lightweight flours. Here are my favourites.

Gluten-free oat flour: For coeliacs oat flour is a little risky unless you are certain your flour is 100 per cent gluten free and no cross contamination has occurred. However, if you aren't allergic to oats, oat flour can provide a great rise and flavour to your baked good. Oat flour can have a gritty texture when used alone so be sure to combine it with another mediumweight flour and one or two lightweight flours to avoid this issue. To save money buy gluten-free oats and grind them in a coffee grinder or food processor to make your own oat flour.

Millet flour: If you are looking for a mildly nutty, wholegrain flavour to your baked good, millet flour is an excellent alternative. Loaded with nutrition, millet flour adds a slight yellow colour to your baking. It's best combined with another mediumweight or heavyweight flour and one or two lightweight flours.

Quinoa flour: Quinoa flour provides a strong earthy, bitter flavour and a protein boost to your baked goods. To remove the bitterness and create better tasting desserts, fill a clean baking tray (baking sheet) with quinoa flour and toast in the oven at 120°C (250°F) for 25–30 minutes, stirring often. When it starts to turn golden and smell toasted, it's ready! It's best combined with another mediumweight or heavyweight flour and one or two lightweight flours.

Sorghum flour: Sorghum flour can mimic the texture of wholemeal (whole-wheat) flour, providing a very soft, light crumb and a wholesome, slightly sweet flavour to your baked good. It's one of my favourite flours and works best when combined with another mediumweight or heavyweight flour and one or two lightweight flours.

White and brown rice flour: These flours are neutral in flavour, easy to work with and provide great structure to your recipe. To avoid a gritty consistency, pulse the flour in a food processor before using to lighten the texture. White and brown rice flour are interchangeable, so use whichever suits you best. I find white rice flour is perfect for shortbreads or recipes with a crumbly texture, and brown rice flour is fantastic for all other uses. They are best combined with another mediumweight or heavyweight flour and one or two lightweight flours.

Heavyweight Flours

Heavyweight flours give structure but don't rise much, making for a dense result. These flours are best combined with lightweight and mediumweight flours. Here are my favourites.

Almond flour: This has a delicious buttery flavour, and adds moisture and a nice kick of protein to your baked good. But it is quite expensive and can be difficult to use alone. It works best when used in small quantities, combined with one or two mediumweight flours and one or two lightweight flours.

Amaranth flour: Perfect for low-rise baked goods, amaranth flour is full of nutrition and provides a distinct, slightly bitter, earthy flavour and dense texture to your recipe. It's best used in combination with one or two mediumweight flours and one or two lightweight flours.

Bean flours: High in protein and fibre, bean flours are fantastic for binding and adding structure to your baked goods. They do, however, leave a very 'beany' taste, so they are better suited to savoury recipes. Combine bean flours with one or two mediumweight flours and one or two lightweight flours for the best result.

Buckwheat flour: Never fear! Despite its name, buckwheat is actually derived from a fruit and not wheat. Carrying an incredible nutritional profile and an earthy flavour, buckwheat flour will provide your recipe with a golden brown hue and a dense texture. You can buy buckwheat flour off the shelf; however, it can have a strong taste and a dark colour, making it unsuitable for desserts.

I like to grind raw buckwheat kernels myself in a food processor or coffee grinder to create flour. This produces a milder-tasting and more delicate flavour for desserts. This flour is best combined with one or two mediumweight flours and one or two lightweight flours.

Coconut flour: Very tricky to use and can be hard to substitute in recipes; I find it works best for thickening sauces or batters. A tablespoon or two will quickly give a wet batter a thick and luscious consistency. Be careful not to add too much as coconut flour will act like a sponge, quickly slurping up any liquid in sight. It can also provide a slightly gritty, dry texture.

I find this flour only works well in small quantities – 30 g (1 oz/¼ cup) or less – and it definitely needs to be combined with one or two heavyweight flours, one or two mediumweight flours and one or two lightweight flours.

Teff flour: A nutty, wholegrain flour that has significant binding qualities but a somewhat overpowering flavour. Use this flour in small quantities and combine with one heavyweight flour, one or two mediumweight flours and one or two lightweight flours.

Create Your Own Gluten-free Flour

GLUTEN FLOUR	GLUTEN-FREE REPLACEMENT
1 kilogram (2 lb 3 oz) flour	150 g (5½ oz) lightweight flour (use 1 or 2 kinds) + 350 g (12½ oz) mediumweight flour (use 1 or 2 kinds) + 350 g (12½ oz) heavyweight flour (use 1 or 2 kinds)
OR	
1 kilogram (2 lb 3 oz) flour	150 g (5½ oz) lightweight flour (use 1 or 2 kinds) + 700 g (1lb 9 oz) mediumweight flour (use 2 kinds)

Whisk flours together in a large bowl and store in a glass jar in the pantry or fridge.

MY GF FLOUR BLEND

This is my go-to gluten-free flour blend, which I have used in the recipes throughout this book unless I have recommended otherwise. It is a fantastic substitute for generic wheat-based plain flour and works well in cakes, cookies, slices, muffins, cupcakes, you name it!

If you are struggling to find sorghum flour, gluten-free oat flour is a great substitute. Just remember to make sure all your flours are 100 per cent gluten free if you have allergies.

Whisk the flour blend together in a large bowl and store in a glass jar.

INGREDIENTS
75 g (2¾ oz) arrowroot starch or tapioca flour
75 g (2¾ oz) potato starch
350 g (12½ oz) sorghum flour
350 g (12½ oz) brown rice flour

GLUTEN REPLACER BLEND

Add ½ teaspoon of this mix per 1 cup of gluten-free flour for bread, scrolls and doughs that rely on a gluten consistency. It can also be used as a substitute for xanthan gum or guar gum in your recipe.

Mix the ingredients together in a large bowl and store in a sealed glass jar.

INGREDIENTS
80 g (2¾ oz) ground chia seeds
80 g (2¾ oz) ground linseeds (flax seeds)
40 g (1½ oz) psyllium husk powder

Gluten-free Baking Tips

Lightness: Increase baking powder and/or bicarbonate of soda (baking soda) by 25 per cent. For example, if the recipe asks for 1 teaspoon of baking powder, add 1¼ teaspoons instead.

Measure everything: I'm not kidding. Now is not the time to throw in a bit of this and a sprinkle of that. Use your kitchen scales to measure everything. No shortcuts!

Sift flour: Sift your flour before adding it to your other ingredients. This will lighten the dessert and provide you with tasty results.

Self-raising (self-rising) flour: Add two teaspoons of baking powder for each 150 g (5½ oz) of gluten-free plain (all-purpose) flour. Sift or whisk flour and baking powder together in a bowl before using for even distribution.

Air: Beat the batter for 2–5 minutes to create air pockets and bring lightness to the end result.

Temperature: Lower your oven temperature by 25°C (77°F), as gluten-free baking tends to brown faster and cook slower on the inside.

Baking time: Add approximately 15 minutes to the recipe time. If the recipe is for 30 minutes and you have converted it to gluten-free, you will often find it takes 45 minutes. Keep a close eye on your baking!

Binding: Most online gluten-free recipes and store-bought gluten-free baked goods will list xanthan gum or guar gum as an ingredient. These gums basically mimic the gluten response in the baked product. However, these two ingredients may cause an upset tummy for sensitive digestive systems. Instead, use the Gluten Replacer Blend listed on page 133 to replace the xanthan or guar gum in any recipe.

Most importantly, HAVE FUN!

Eggs & Oil.

This chapter isn't to preach a fear of fat. Nor will it provide weight loss tips or ways to make your baking fat free. Oil can perform an important function, ensuring recipes stay moist and rich during the cooking process. But, even better, it can be replaced with beneficial substitutes.

Eggs are considered critical in baking: they bind ingredients, prevent crumbling and encourage your dessert to rise. They're the key to making super light and fluffy spoonfuls. When substituting eggs, it's essential to take a closer look at the recipe. This will help you decide if the eggs' role is for binding or leavening.

There are a few quick ways to make this decision. Read on.

Binding

Eggs in desserts can act as a binder, holding your ingredients together while cooking to prevent crumbling.

If the recipe includes eggs plus raising agents, such as baking powder, bicarbonate of soda (baking soda) or baker's yeast, the eggs will help bind the ingredients together.

Leavening

Eggs can also provide air to dessert batters, allowing them to rise. If the recipe calls for no raising agents, but lists ingredients such as vinegar, citrus juice or buttermilk, then the eggs will help the recipe rise.

The fewer eggs required in a recipe, the easier it will be to substitute.

Alternatives to Eggs & Oil

Aquafaba

Best for: meringues, pavlovas, macarons, baked goods

How to: Unless the recipe says otherwise, whisk the aquafaba until it's frothy, then incorporate into your recipe.

1 medium egg white = 2 tablespoons of aquafaba

Tips: Aquafaba is the water in which legumes have been cooked. Yes, you heard right — it's the water that usually goes down the sink when we drain our tinned beans. When you whisk this bean juice it mimics the functional properties of egg whites, thus making a fantastic plant-based substitute in meringue recipes!

Avoid the salted tinned varieties, or your recipe will taste very beany and have a strong smell. Look for chickpeas in water or white beans in water as the two main (or only) ingredients.

Beans

Best for: brownies, cakes, muffins

How to: Purée 400 g (14 oz) of salt-free tinned beans (chickpeas, white beans and black beans work best) in a high-speed blender (bean liquid and all).

Bean purée can replace 75 per cent of added oil in a recipe. Replace the other 25 per cent with yoghurt for the best results.

Tips: The plant fibre found in beans will naturally improve the texture of low-fat baked goods, making them dense and fudgy. Their high fibre content will also fill up your stomach and slow the rush of sugar to your bloodstream after consuming. I like to use black beans in chocolate recipes, and white beans in lighter-coloured baked goods.

Beans can make your baking denser, so for best results use them in fudgy recipes, such as brownies or mudcakes, and always use a salt-free variety to avoid a bean-scented dessert.

Bicarbonate of Soda (Baking Soda)

Best for: muffins, cakes, bread

How to: 1 egg (leavening) = 1 teaspoon of bicarbonate of soda + 1 tablespoon of lemon juice or vinegar, mixed well

Tips: Bicarbonate of soda will add a fluffy and light texture to your baked good and is fantastic for leavening. However, too much bicarbonate of soda will add a bitter flavour to your recipe — so it's important to use this method when only one egg is required.

Chia Seeds/Linseeds (Flaxseeds)

Best for: brownies, cakes, muffins, raw desserts, loaves

How to: 1 egg (binding) = 1 tablespoon of chia seeds or linseeds + 3 tablespoons of water

1 egg (leavening) = 1 tablespoon of chia seeds or linseeds + 3 tablespoons of water + ¼ teaspoon of baking powder

1 egg yolk = 1 tablespoon of chia seeds or linseeds + 2 tablespoons of water

250 ml (8½ fl oz/1 cup) of oil = 190 ml (6½ fl oz/¾ cup) of water or other liquid + 4 tablespoons of chia seeds or linseeds

Tips: When ground into flour or used in their whole form, chia seeds and linseeds help bind other ingredients in the recipe, preventing crumbling and dry desserts.

Whole chia seeds or linseeds can be ground in a coffee grinder or food processor if you don't have the ground variety on hand. Store ground chia seeds and linseeds in the fridge.

Cornflour (Cornstarch) or Arrowroot Starch

Best for: cookies, muffins, brownies, bread

How to: 1 egg (binding) = 1 tablespoon of starch + 2 tablespoons of water

Tips: These starches will help bind ingredients together and produce a moist, dense texture. Keep in mind they won't provide any rise to your baked good.

If more than one egg is required, use this in combination with another egg substitute. Always check the cornflour is gluten free and non-GMO.

Fruit or Vegetable Purée

Best for: brownies, cakes, muffins, cookies, bars

How to: 1 egg (binding or leavening) = 60 g (2 oz/¼ cup) of purée (approximately) + ½ teaspoon of bicarbonate of soda (baking soda)

250 ml (8½ fl oz/1 cup) of oil = 180 g (6½ oz/¾ cup) of purée (approximately)

Tips: Purées can add moisture to your recipe and prevent it from drying out or crumbling. My favourite purées include unsweetened apple sauce, pear, avocado, banana, pumpkin, beetroot (beet) and sweet potato. Pumpkin, sweet potato, beetroot and apple need to be cooked before puréeing.

Remember: the stronger the flavour of purée, the more you will be able to taste it in the final result. Be sure to match your purée to your recipe flavours.

Check your oven about 10 minutes prior to completion time, as you may find that recipes cook faster with a fruit or vegetable purée. Avoid using more than 240 g (9 oz/1 cup) of purée in any recipe.

Nut or Seed Butter

Best for: raw treats, unbaked goods

How to: Chilled nut or seed butters can be swapped 1:1 cup in recipes that ask for a solid fat. If your recipe asks for a liquefied fat, you can use any of the other replacements in this section.

Tips: Nut or seed butters boast an abundance of nutrients per serve and can stand in for solid fat in a recipe. Always make your own nut or seed butter at home or choose natural varieties with no added sugars, salt or trans fats. My top picks are almond, cashew nut and tahini.

Prunes or Dried Dates

Best for: brownies, chocolate cake, chocolate muffins, chocolate cookies

How to: Add 220 g (8 oz/1½ cups) of pitted prunes or pitted dates to a food processor or blender with 100 ml (3½ fl oz/⅓ cup) of water. Pulse until it forms a purée.

250 ml (8½ fl oz/1 cup) of oil = 280 g (10 oz/1 cup) of prune or date purée + 1–2 tablespoons of water or plant-based milk

Tips: Loaded with vitamins, prunes and dates provide a low-fat alternative to oil and work extremely well in chocolate baked goods. They will keep your baking soft yet crisp on the outside, just like oil!

Silken Tofu

Best for: brownies, cakes, muffins

How to: 1 egg (binding) = 50 g (1¾ oz/¼ cup) of puréed silken tofu + ¼ teaspoon of bicarbonate of soda (baking soda)

1 egg yolk = 25 g (1 oz/⅛ cup) of puréed silken tofu

Replace half the oil in the recipe with tofu and the other half with fruit or vegetable purée for a healthy treat!

Tips: Tofu has a very mild flavour that almost disappears in baked goods, while it adds a protein and calcium boost to each bite.

Keep in mind that soy is a common allergen, so if you are cooking for others another substitute may suit better. Always choose organic, non-GMO soy products to avoid potential toxins.

Yoghurt

Best for: brownies, cakes, muffins, loaves

How to: 1 egg (binding) = 60 g (2 oz/¼ cup) of yoghurt

1 egg yolk = 30 g (1 oz/⅛ cup) of yoghurt

250 ml (8½ fl oz/1 cup) of oil = 185 g (6½ oz/¾ cup) of yoghurt

Tips: Yoghurt can keep cakes from tasting overly sweet and provide a dense and homemade feel. I like to use coconut yoghurt to give richness to desserts.

If your yoghurt is overly watery try draining it in a very fine-mesh strainer before adding it to your recipes.

Zucchini (Courgettes)

Best for: cakes, loaves, muffins

How to: 250 ml (8½ fl oz/1 cup) of oil = 135 g (5 oz/1 cup) of shredded zucchini

Tips: Full of vitamin C, fibre, magnesium, vitamin A and potassium, zucchini is a fantastic alternative to oil and produces naturally moist results similar to oil in baking. Peel the zucchini and shred with a grater. Children won't even know it has been used in your baking.

Egg Conversion

BINDING REPLACEMENT	TO REPLACE 1 EGG	TIPS
Chia seeds or linseeds (flaxseeds)	1 tablespoon + 3 tablespoons water	
Cornflour (cornstarch) or arrowroot starch or tapioca flour	1 tablespoon + 2 tablespoons water	If more than 1 egg is required, use in combination with another substitute
Fruit or vegetable purée	60 g (2 oz/¼ cup approximately) + ½ teaspoon of bicarbonate of soda (baking soda)	
Puréed silken tofu	50 g (1¾ oz/¼ cup) + ¼ teaspoon of bicarbonate of soda (baking soda)	
Yoghurt	60 g (2 oz/¼ cup)	

LEAVENING REPLACEMENT	TO REPLACE 1 EGG	TIPS
Bicarbonate of soda (baking soda)	1 teaspoon + 1 tablespoon of lemon juice or vinegar	I find apple cider vinegar or lemon juice works best
Chia seeds Linseeds (flaxseeds)	1 tablespoon + 3 tablespoons of water + ¼ teaspoon of bicarbonate of soda (baking soda)	
Fruit or vegetable purée	60 g (2 oz/¼ cup) approximately + ½ teaspoon of bicarbonate of soda (baking soda)	

EGG WHITE REPLACEMENT	TO REPLACE 1 EGG WHITE	TIPS
Aquafaba (chickpea or bean cooking water)	2 tablespoons	Whisk mixture until frothy before use

EGG YOLK REPLACEMENT	TO REPLACE 1 EGG YOLK	
Chia seeds or linseeds (flaxseeds)	1 tablespoon + 2 tablespoons of water	
Silken tofu	25 g (1 oz/⅛ cup)	
Yoghurt	30 g (1 oz/⅛ cup)	

Oil Conversion

LIQUID OIL REPLACEMENT	TO REPLACE 1 CUP
Bean purée	175 g (6 oz/¾ cup) + 60 g (2 oz/¼ cup) yoghurt
Chia seeds or linseeds (flax seeds)	4 tablespoons + 190 ml (6½ fl oz/¾ cup) water or other liquid
Fruit or vegetable purée	180 g (6½ oz/¾ cup) approximately
Prune or date purée	280 g (10 oz/1 cup) + 1–2 tablespoons liquid
Shredded zucchini (courgette)	135 g (5 oz/1 cup)
Silken tofu	100 g (3½ oz/½ cup) + 120 g (4½ oz/½ cup) fruit or vegetable purée
Yoghurt	185 g (6½ oz/¾ cup)

SOLID OIL REPLACEMENT	TO REPLACE 1 CUP
Coconut cream	250 ml (8½ fl oz/1 cup) nut or seed butter
Nut or seed butter	250 g (9 oz/1 cup)

Dairy.

Milk has long been the go-to source for creamy, rich desserts. Thick dollops of cream, smoothness in chocolate and crumbling textures in a shortcrust are all qualities produced by using dairy products. Milk is everywhere, and for anyone with an intolerance it feels difficult to avoid.

Luckily, the best alternatives are never far from reach. I'm a big fan of coconut milk, coconut cream and coconut yoghurt. With one simple ingredient, you'll be able to mimic the richness and texture of dairy.

Alternatives to Dairy

Coconut Milk

Best for: custards, fudges, sauces, pie fillings

How to: Refrigerate a tin of coconut milk overnight. After opening, you will notice the coconut cream has risen to the top and the coconut water is left on the bottom.

Swap evaporated milk 1:1 cup for coconut milk, and swap cream 1:1 cup for solidified coconut cream. If you use an electric mixer and beat the solidified coconut cream it will transform into whipped cream just like its dairy alternative.

Tips: Coconut milk can provide a replacement for cream and evaporated milk in one tin! It will enhance the flavours in your recipe and provide a creamy consistency. Look for full-fat tinned coconut milk made from the meat of the coconut and with only two ingredients: coconut and water.

Coconut Yoghurt and Silken Tofu

Best for: cakes, loaves, muffins, cupcakes

How to: 250 g (9 oz/1 cup) of yoghurt = 250 g (9 oz/1 cup) of coconut yoghurt

250 g (9 oz/1 cup) of yoghurt = 200 g (7 oz/1 cup) of puréed silken tofu

Tips: Coconut yoghurt, silken tofu and vegan buttermilk (see page 152) can adequately substitute yoghurt in recipes to provide moisture and richness to the dish. If you are using yoghurt to serve with your recipe, choose coconut yoghurt for a luxurious cream alternative.

Crumbled Firm Tofu

Best for: cakes, cheesecakes, savoury dishes

How to: 250 g (9 oz/1 cup) of cottage cheese or ricotta cheese = 120 g (4½ oz/1 cup) of crumbled tofu

Tips: I find cottage cheese and ricotta cheese lack substance but come alive when you add different flavour combinations to them. Crumbled firm tofu is a great substitute when your recipe asks for cottage cheese or ricotta cheese. It provides the creaminess without adding an overpowering flavour.

Remember to always choose organic soy products free from genetic modification and unnecessary chemicals.

Plant-based Condensed Milk

Best for: decadent slices, cakes and raw treats

How to: 315 g (11 oz/1 cup) of condensed milk = 315 g (11 oz/1 cup) of coconut condensed milk

315 g (11 oz/1 cup) of condensed milk = 315 g (11 oz/1 cup) of soy condensed milk

Tips: Substitute traditional condensed milk 1:1 cup with coconut or soy condensed milk. You will hardly notice the difference in your decadent dessert!

Plant-based Ice Cream

Best for: Any dessert!

How to: Swap coconut or soy ice cream 1:1 cup for dairy ice cream.

Tips: The creamy, melt-in-your-mouth spoonful of ice cream doesn't have to be lost to those we can't eat dairy. Lots of coconut and soy-based ice creams are readily available from most supermarkets and health food stores. If not, make your own (page 100)!

If you don't like the taste of coconut, don't use coconut ice cream. I find that it doesn't matter which flavour you buy — there will always be a hint of coconut lingering in the background. If you make your own ice cream it's best consumed within a day or two to avoid an icy texture.

Plant-based Milk

Best for: cakes, cookies, slices, pies, tarts

How to: Swap plant-based milk 1:1 cup for dairy milk.

Tips: Plant-based milks create a soft batter or dough while retaining structure and rising properties. You can substitute milk in recipes with any plant-based milk, fruit juice or yoghurt you desire. Choose flavours you love as you may notice a small difference in taste depending on which milk you use.

I find rice, almond, coconut or soy milk best for sweet treats. Always look for milk with the smallest amount of additives, or make your own at home.

Plant-based Yoghurt

Best for: cakes, muffins, bread

How to: 250 g (9 oz/1 cup) of sour cream = 250 g (9 oz/1 cup) of plant-based yoghurt

250 g (9 oz/1 cup) of sour cream = 190 ml (6½ fl oz/¾ cup) of coconut yoghurt + 1 tablespoon of vinegar or lemon juice

Tips: Plant-based yoghurt is my favourite substitute for sour cream as it provides the rich flavour and creaminess we all desire. Always use full-fat yoghurt when replacing sour cream to avoid the added thickeners and stabilisers, and always add it to a sauce after you have taken it off the heat to avoid splitting. Remember coconut yoghurt has a slight tang and a strong coconut taste compared to sour cream, so it's important to adjust your flavours accordingly.

You can also use coconut milk plus vinegar as a sour cream substitute. It works well but has a thinner consistency than traditional sour cream.

Solidified Coconut Cream

Best for: cakes, cookies, slices

How to: 250 g (9 oz/1 cup) of butter = 220 g (8 oz/1 cup) of coconut cream (solidified)

Refrigerate a tin of coconut milk overnight. Once cold, the coconut cream will solidify and rise to the top, leaving the coconut water below. Swap the butter in your recipe 1:1 with the solidified coconut cream.

If the recipe calls for softened butter, let the cold solid coconut cream sit at room temperature before using. If the recipe asks for melted butter, melt the solid coconut cream over a low heat. If the recipe requests whipped butter, beat the solid coconut cream with a mixer or by hand.

Tips: Solidified coconut cream can be used as a fantastic flavourful replacement for butter to give moistness, and a light and airy texture to baked goods. The only downfall is it won't work as well for shortbreads, which rely on that real butter flavour.

When making solidified coconut cream, always look for full-fat tinned coconut milk made from the meat of the coconut and with only two ingredients: coconut and water. Light coconut milk contains less of the coconut flesh and often doesn't work as well for creaming or whipping.

Soy Cream Cheese

Best for: A dollop or spread here and there!

How to: Strain coconut, soy or lactose-free yoghurt overnight in the fridge by tying it up in either cheesecloth or a nut-milk bag and hanging it to drain over a glass jar or bowl. This will eliminate any liquid and create a robust, creamy cheese. In the morning, discard the liquid and use your creamy mock cheese in your recipe of choice.

Swap strained cheese 1:1 for cream cheese.

Tips: You can buy soy-based cream cheese off the shelf, but I find it's always best to create your own to avoid the nasty additives. Strained yoghurt will provide a thick, creamy texture similar to cream cheese.

Remember that it's important to choose a yoghurt with a natural or Greek flavour for the optimal cream cheese texture. You can choose coconut yoghurt — however, it will have a strong coconut taste after straining.

Vegan Buttermilk

Best for: bread, cakes, loaves, muffins

How to: 250 ml (8½ fl oz/1 cup) of buttermilk = 250 ml (8½ fl oz/1 cup) of plant-based milk + 1 tablespoon of vinegar or lemon juice

Tips: The easiest to substitute in recipes, buttermilk can be made vegan by using plant-based milk and adding lemon juice or vinegar. It may not curdle like regular dairy-based buttermilk, but it will still serve the same purpose in a recipe. It can also be swapped 1:1 cup for yoghurt in a recipe.

For best results, allow the vinegar and milk mixture to rest for at least 10 minutes before adding to your recipe. I love using apple cider vinegar.

Dairy Conversion

DAIRY SOURCE	SWAPS
Butter	Coconut butter Coconut oil Nut or seed butter Vegan butter
Buttermilk	250 ml (8½ fl oz/1 cup) plant-based milk + 1 tablespoon of vinegar or lemon juice
Condensed milk	Coconut condensed milk Soy condensed milk
Cottage cheese/ Ricotta cheese	Crumbled firm tofu
Cream	Coconut cream Coconut yoghurt
Cream cheese	Cheese from strained yoghurt
Evaporated milk	Coconut milk
Ice cream	Coconut ice cream Soy ice cream
Milk	Almond milk Coconut milk Macadamia nut milk Oat milk Rice milk Soy milk Other plant-based milk Fruit juice Plant-based yoghurt
Sour cream	190 ml (6½ fl oz/¾ cup) plant-based milk + 1 tablespoon of vinegar or lemon juice 250 g (9 oz/1 cup) plant-based yoghurt
Yoghurt	Coconut yoghurt Silken tofu Vegan buttermilk

Nuts.

So many classic desserts demand a crunch factor. It's the perfect marriage of sweet and gooey, with a surprising explosion of crunch. Nuts are a fantastic source of texture, and you can butter them, candy them, roast and toast them.

Before we begin, identify the difference between personal taste and nut allergy. If you don't like the taste of certain nuts, explore the alternatives listed in this chapter. If you're subject to anaphylactic shock, don't experiment or push the boundaries. Stick to what you know and always be sure to check ingredient lists for any triggers.

Nut Conversion

NUT SOURCE	SWAPS
Almonds	Crushed gluten-free biscuits Gluten-free oats Hazelnuts Peanuts Sunflower kernels
Cashew nuts	Fresh coconut meat Macadamia nuts Shredded coconut
Hazelnuts	Almonds Buckwheat kernels Sunflower kernels
Macadamia nuts	Cashew nuts Pepitas (pumpkin seeds) Shredded coconut Sunflower kernels
Nut butter	Coconut butter Seed butter
Peanuts	Almonds Buckwheat kernels Crushed gluten-free biscuits Sunflower kernels
Pecans	Crushed gluten-free biscuits Gluten-free oats Sunflower kernels Walnuts
Pine nuts	Pepitas (pumpkin seeds) Sesame seeds Shredded coconut Sunflower kernels
Walnuts	Crushed gluten-free biscuits Gluten-free oats Pecans Sunflower kernels

INDEX

A BIG THANK YOU
FROM THE HEART

In creating this book, I've been honoured to work with some of the most inspirational and talented people in my life today. Their guidance and creative influence have revamped my humble first hard-copy book into the beautiful pocket book you're holding now.

First and foremost, a huge thank you to Jeremy. Not only are you my husband, but my forever soulmate, best friend, business partner and self-declared number-one fan. With you, I've built this life I adore, created a community I treasure, and shaped the confidence to share my soul with the world. Your endless late nights designing, taking photos and bravely taste testing never go unnoticed. I am the luckiest woman in the world to have you and our new baby boy, Jonah, by my side. I love you with every inch of my being, and I thank you so much.

Pam Brewster, the wonderful woman who has believed in me for many years. Thank you for taking the time to brainstorm ideas for this new and improved book. Your support means the world and *Sweet Vegan* would not be a reality without you.

Thank you, Loran McDougall, Marg Bowman and Allison Hiew, for your patience and guidance throughout this journey. You were my trusted eyes, voice, ears and mind. Loran, your attention to detail when creating *Sweet Vegan* was very much appreciated, as I was battling little sleep with a newborn and baby brain. You are wonderful.

Michelle Mackintosh, Mietta Yans and Susanne Geppert, my lovely, talented designers. Thank you for creating a book I will cherish for the rest of my life.

A special thanks to Elisa Watson, my incredible photographer, and Georgia Young, my superb food stylist. Your love of food and infinite knowledge was truly appreciated. You never failed to plate perfection and capture those precious moments. Thank you for all your hard work; I look forward to working with you both again in the future.

To all the lovely people at Hardie Grant, thank you for working with me. From the moment I met you, your approachability and caring nature warmed my heart. You're a dream to work with and I couldn't have picked a better team to collaborate with. Thank you for being a part of my journey and I am truly grateful for everything you do.

With great affection and gratitude, I would like to thank my family and friends. You have all helped shape the person I am today with your endless support, love, understanding and honest taste testing. You encourage me to be the best version of myself, and I love having you all by my side on this wondrous journey. I hope to shower you all with healthy sweet treats over the coming years.

Most importantly, a big warm thank you goes to you, for following my journey, connecting with me daily, supporting my blog and purchasing this new book. I hope to continuously provide you with a spark of inspiration in the kitchen and motivation to try something new. I urge you to share this book with your friends. Reclaim these recipes as your own. Brag about sweet potato icing to everyone you meet. Try something new and always remember to bring joy, love and soul to each plate because beautiful food can create a memory that lasts forever.

Nicole Maree x